D0929843

THE TEACH YOURSELF BOOKS

LOGIC

Uniform with this volume
and in the same series

TEACH YOURSELF

LOGIC

A. A. LUCE
M.C., D.D., Litt.D.

THE ENGLISH UNIVERSITIES PRESS LTD
ST. PAUL'S HOUSE WARWICK LANE
LONDON EC4

First printed 1958
This impression 1968

SBN 340 05645 2

*Printed in Great Britain for the English Universities Press Ltd
by Butler & Tanner Ltd, Frome and London*

PREFACE

Logic can be taught in various ways, and a teacher soon finds by experience the method that best suits his own style. The following hints are for those who are teaching themselves from this textbook. The book follows the natural articulations of the subject-matter, and it can be read through solidly from beginning to end. For beginners, however, I recommend the selective reading, indicated below, which concentrates first on the outline structure or skeleton of syllogistic Logic, before going on to the complete, continuous reading. This plan of reading keeps the *structure* of Logic steadily before the learner's eye ; the details are seen in perspective, and the skeleton is gradually clothed with flesh and blood.

The plan would work out as follows : Glance through the first chapter and get the general notion. From Chapters II, III, IV, and V select pages 12–18, 34–55, and 64–95 for slow, patient, and thorough study. Do exercises as you go along, your own or from those printed at the end of the chapter. Understand as you read, and do not read far ahead of what you have understood. From these selections you will learn enough about terms to understand the structure of the proposition, and enough about propositions to grasp the structure of the syllogism, and enough about syllogisms to be able to prove the Special Rules of the Figures. When you can prove those rules with ease, you have grasped the outline structure and skeleton of syllogistic Logic.

That done, go back to Chapter I and read the whole book continuously. The gaps will now close. The sections on the technical classifications of terms, and non-categorical propositions, etc., omitted at the first reading, will now come easily to you, and you can pass on to the study of the Moods and Reduction, and thence to the more miscellaneous contents of Chapters VII and VIII. Chapters IX and X point on to more advanced studies and should be left for the last.

May reminiscence be permitted here and a piece of personal experience? I taught myself Logic in my youth from a small old-fashioned manual. It was not written for logicians, but for the non-specialized pass-man, and without unnecessary technicalities or trimmings it set out the basic and timeless truths of traditional Logic, some knowledge of which is essential, in my opinion, to a consciously correct and rational use of our mother-tongue.

I found the subject difficult at first; it was not like any of my school subjects; but when I had crossed the threshold, an inner door swung open. I took a step forward in self-knowledge, and thought and speech became self-conscious. Like Molière's M. Jourdain who found that he had long been speaking prose, I found that I had long been forming propositions. I said to myself, "Yes, I form propositions when my tongue does more than wag. I form them out of terms. I say something *about* something. Therefore I ought to be able, in serious talk, to pin-point those two parts of my proposition. I ought to know exactly what I am talking about, and exactly what I am saying about it." Soon inference, too, became self-conscious. From a child I had inferred and reasoned; now I began to do so wittingly, aware of the traps and the pitfalls, and aware of a norm and an ideal.

In lecturing on Logic to University men and women, over and over again I have seen the same door swing open, the same step forward taken, the same marked development. The nerveless, juvenile letter written to the College Tutor twelve months previously, has now turned into a logical, well-knit communication, its subject-matter thought out, its phrasing clear and concise. Logic can do this for you. Other maturing influences there are, of course, but Logic can open that inner door of the mind and promote that advance in self-knowledge ; and in doing so Logic is living up to its historic title, the *Organon* or Instrument of knowledge.

Our Logic is the lineal descendant of the *ars logica*, one of the three introductory disciplines that constituted the *trivium* which was the groundwork of education in the Middle Ages. The traditional place of Logic in our curriculum is that of a *propaedeutic* or preliminary discipline, a non-specialist introduction to general culture and knowledge ; and for the non-specialized student the traditional place of Logic is still the correct place.

Recent developments of Logic go far afield, and may make the traditional Logic seem narrow in range and scope. That narrowness is more apparent than real ; for a little key can open a large door. Or should we say that the ' narrowness ' of Aristotelian Logic is part of its *raison d'être* ? Its primary purpose is not to impart information about Logic, or about the logic of Logic, or about any other subject, but to drill and discipline the young thinker's mind and discourse ; and drill and discipline are best taught within the narrow bounds of the parade-ground.

I am much indebted to *An Introduction to Logic* by H. W. B. Joseph ; references are to the second edition, revised, 1916. References to Aristotle are to the Oxford translation, ed. W. D. Ross, vol. I, 1928. I have consulted *The Elements of Logic* by T. K. Abbott, 1883, *Principles of*

Logic by G. H. Joyce, 3rd ed. 1920, *Studies and Exercises in Formal Logic* by J. N. Keynes, 1928, *General Logic* by R. M. Eaton, 1931, *Fundamentals of Symbolic Logic* by A. Ambrose and M. Lazerowitz, 1950, and *Introduction to Symbolic Logic*, by A. H. Basson and D. J. O'Connor, 1953. From the last-mentioned work, now in the second edition, I have taken below (pp. 203–4) Chapter and Section headings to indicate the scope of elementary Symbolic Logic, as it is taught today, and I am obliged to the publishers, University Tutorial Press Ltd., and to the authors, Messrs. Basson and O'Connor, for permission to do so.

I thank my colleagues, Mr. F. La T. Godfrey, Mr. W. V. Denard, and my son Mr. J. V. Luce, who read the work in typescript and advised on it, Professor D. A. Webb for his help with the section on the methodology of Plant Biology, Professor W. D. Gill for recasting the section on turbidity currents, and Professor E. J. Furlong for reading the proofs and for his valuable suggestions.

A. A. Luce

Trinity College, Dublin

CONTENTS

A*

CHAPTER I

THE STUDY OF LOGIC

THE word *Logic* comes from the Greek λόγος, which means *discourse*. The study of Logic began in ancient Greece when men set to work to master the guiding principles of discourse, and Logic still is a discipline of discourse. Wherever men debate, discuss, and argue, Logic is a court of appeal in the background ; whenever a man debates a matter in his own mind, a silent Logic arbitrates. No man in his senses will willingly and persistently defy a clear verdict by Logic. Whoever sets out to break Logic, as has been said, Logic will break him. For many centuries the study of Logic was an essential preliminary of higher education, and it has left a deep and lasting mark on the language and outlook of cultured men. Logic is in the air we breathe. Many still study it with profit, and many who have not time to study it for themselves benefit unconsciously from the logical labours of past generations.

Discourse is connected thought, expressed in words. It moves this way and that, like the shuttle in the loom (as Plato said), weaving the fabric of reasoned argument. In discourse with others opinion is formed, knowledge is acquired, and truth attained. What is said by one speaker, combined with what is said by another speaker, may yield a truth, not previously known to either speaker. In that discourse with oneself which is called reflection or meditation, a truth learned today links up with a truth learned yesterday, and the two truths may point the way to some advance or even discovery of tomorrow. From what others have said or from what we ourselves have thought, conclusions and inferences are drawn, and they are the special concern of Logic. It is all too easy to draw wrong conclusions and false inferences; and discourse without the discipline of Logic is a fruitful source of false opinion, ignorance, and error.

Logic trains the mind to draw the right conclusion, and to avoid the wrong, to make the true inference and not the false. It has formulated rules of inference to govern and guide debate and to promote discovery. Logic has to deal as well with other important elements of discourse, but its main province has always been, and still is, Inference.

Truth and Validity

Idle talk and trivial conversation do not rank as *discourse* for our purpose. Logic has little to do with the frivolous; its business is with the serious statement which admits truth or falsity.[1] Logic promotes truth; yet we can go far in Logic without knowing or caring much whether a particular statement is true or false, in the ordinary acceptation of those words. By *true* in ordinary speech we mean *true to fact*, and by *false* we mean the opposite. Now a statement, true to fact, may in its context infringe a rule of Logic; and a statement, false in fact, may in its context conform to the rules of Logic. The logician, as such, is not directly concerned with fact, but is much concerned with the observance of the rules of Logic, and therefore he uses a pair of technical terms, *valid* and *invalid*, to express, respectively, what conforms to the rules of Logic, and what

[1] " Propositions as have in them either truth or falsity . . ." Aristotle, *De Interpretatione*, ch. 4, 17a.

does not conform thereto. By aid of these terms he can set out the rules of reasoning without committing himself as to whether a particular statement is true to fact, or not. *Valid* comes from the Latin, *validus*, strong. A valid passport may make mistakes in fact, but if duly signed and not out of date, it may do its work and get you through the barrier. On the other hand, it may give the colour of the eyes and all the other facts correctly, but if it is out of date, it will not do its work; it is invalid. The distinction between *truth* and *validity* must be carefully observed. It is illogical and therefore incorrect to speak of a *true* syllogism, if you mean a *valid* syllogism, or of a *valid* conclusion, if you mean a *true* conclusion.

Form and Content

Logic is *Formal Logic*; it studies the *form* of discourse. The opposite of form is *content* or *subject-matter*. We think and speak of many things; the forms employed are relatively few and fixed. Consider the three sentences:

> Man is mortal.
> The whale is a mammal.
> The grass is green.

They are similar in form; in content they differ widely. One is about human mortality; one is about the classing of whales, and the third about the colour of grass. Logic has nothing to teach about mortality or grass or whales, but has much to teach about the form, called propositional, which the three sentences have in common. Men discuss religion, ethics, politics, and the *why* and the *wherefore* of this, that, and the other. Whatever they happen to be thinking and speaking about, their discourse, like the shuttle in the loom, pursues a set course or track. That course or track is the *form* that Logic studies. Logical form is the common and constant element in precision-thinking. We may picture *form* as a course or track or framework, or as a mould that shapes the jelly ; but the most comprehensive account of it is furnished by the Table of Contents on page ix, which tells what this book is about. It is about terms, propositions, syllogisms, concepts, judgments, inferences, hypothetical and disjunctive arguments, dilemmas, etc.—all that constitutes the *form* of discourse ; in those ways man's discursive thinking proceeds.

Form and Formalism

Formal Logic need not become formalist, and it loses touch, if it does. We are not studying dead words, but living discourse. For instance, the word *and* is no mere connective form. ' Three and two make five ' is the same mathematically as ' Two and three make five ' ; but ' He learned Logic and died ' is not the same as ' He died and learned Logic.' For in discourse *and* involves *sequence*. *Form* in Logic must be kept in touch with Content ; the two are distinct, yet inseparable, like concave and convex. The most nimble thinker cannot think about nothing, and if we had nothing to think about there would be no thought at all. We can separate cream from milk ; we cannot separate the *form* of discourse from its *content*.

Francis Bacon compared Logic to athletics,[1] and an illustration from athletics may help readers to master this delicate distinction. Every athlete knows what it is to

---

[1] " A kind of athletic art to strengthen the sinews of the understanding." Bacon, *Novum Organum*, Preface.

be above or below *form*. Athletic form is a real thing, distinct from performance on the field, yet inseparable from it. *Form* in cricket is taught at the nets. At the nets there are no runs to be scored ; there the coach cares little how hard the batsman hits, or how far the ball would travel. The coach watches how the batsman places his feet and holds his bat and faces the bowling. He teaches *form*, not run-getting, and stance, grip, and concentration *are* batting-form. If the coach can correct, improve, and perfect this form, the runs and centuries and victories will come all in good time, when the nets are rolled up, and the real game is on. But here, as also in Logic, the distinction is no division. Cricket form is inseparable from the matter of the game. Good batting-form is no good, unless it issues in good cuts, and glances and drives, etc. Stance and grip affect the placing and timing and power of the stroke, and the stroke reacts upon the stance and grip.

The point of the illustration is this. In the pages that follow we take the form of discourse seriously and systematically, pointing out the correct forms, as does the coach at the nets, and giving warning of the incorrect ; but we do not make a clean cut between form and content, nor study form for form's sake. The objects about which we think and speak affect the forms of thought and speech employed, and training in the right use of these forms must not ignore their content, but must have an eye to the all-round improvement of discourse itself.

Historical

The demand for Logic arose in ancient Greece from the Sophistic movement. The Sophists were the pioneers of

higher education, and they taught largely by 'disputations'[1] in study circles.   Their disputations required rules
for regulating discussion and formulating agreed conclusions.   Logic supplied the rules, taking up where
grammar left off.   The historic connection between Logic
and grammar should be noted.   Many of the distinctions
and definitions, contained in Logic, are little more than
higher grammar ; and that is as it should be ; for Logic
and grammar both deal with discourse, and the one
discipline shades off into the other.

Adumbrations of Logic are found in Plato's works ;[2]
but, by and large, the science of logic was founded by
one man, Aristotle of Stagira (384–322 B.C.).   Aristotle
was the son of a Macedonian physician at the court of
Amyntas II, the father of Philip of Macedon.   At the age
of seventeen Aristotle went to Athens and there for
twenty years he studied at Plato's Academy, as pupil and
associate.   On Plato's death he left Athens, and taught
for a time at Assos.   Invited by Philip of Macedon to
Pella, he spent seven years there, and amongst his pupils
was Philip's son, Alexander the Great.   When Alexander
came to the throne, Aristotle returned to Athens, and set
up his own school or university, known as the Lyceum.

Aristotle was one of the greatest thinkers of all time,
and he wrote on most of the sciences, known in his day.
His writings on Logic include, (1) the *Prior Analytics*,
which deals mainly with the formal aspect of syllogistic
reasoning, (2) the *Posterior Analytics*, which treats of the

---

[1] Cf. " Disputing daily in the school of one Tyrannus ", Acts xix 9,
cf. *ib.* xvii 17.

[2] The method of enquiry by hypothesis, *Phaedo*, 99d–101e, cf.
Republic, 511b, 533a–d, and *Parmenides*, 135d–136c ; the principle
of contradiction, *Republic*, 436b ; subject and predicate, *Sophist*,
261d ff. ; *genus* and *species*, *Sophist*, 218b ff. ; denotation and connotation, *Theaetetus*, 146c–148d.

deeper problems of inference, and (3) the *Topics*, which deals with the technique of establishing and refuting arguments. These works with some minor pieces received the title of 'Aristotle's Organon' (or Organum,[1] i.e. instrument); for Logic is not an end in itself, but is a means or instrument for fitting the mind to acquire knowledge in any branch of the humanities or science.

Aristotle was the first to see the problem of Logic as a whole, and in large measure he found the solution. He has left the door open for extensions and developments, but certainly the Logic of discourse which from his day to ours has been the accepted *Instrument* of European culture sprang full-grown from Aristotle's teeming mind, like Pallas Athene in the legend from the head of Zeus.

The study of *Logic* and Natural Logic

Aristotle's achievement is without a parallel. Other great men have founded sciences, and the sciences have matured gradually, several minds contributing. Aristotle virtually completed the Logic that he began. The results have been some good, some bad. It is good that there should be a compact, consistent body of doctrine, like Aristotelian Logic, handed down from generation to generation, relatively unchanged, on a subject that from the nature of the case does not change, with a great name guaranteeing the goods; for Logic proper[2] is still in

[1] Hence Francis Bacon, who thought he had discovered a new logic, entitled his famous book *Novum Organum*, i.e. the New Instrument.

[2] By 'Logic proper' is meant Logic in the historic sense of the word, unqualified by adjectives, such as 'symbolic', which are used to express later developments of Logic. Historic claims are generally recognized in such matters, but the extension of the term is of course quite legitimate.

essence Aristotelian Logic. It is good that there should
be unity and continuity in higher education and the
approaches to general culture. But a price has been paid,
and some may think it high. An *undue* deference to the
authority of Aristotle has resulted. That is a bad thing.
It has meant that such mistakes in Logic as Aristotle made
were slow to be corrected. It has meant that too much
has been claimed for his Logic, and too much expected
from it. Men pass readily from one extreme to the other.
Excessive claims and expectations provoke violent reactions, and Aristotle's Logic has been from time to time
a target for attack. By and large, however, it stands
unshaken; it still serves the modest purpose for which it
was designed; and no substitute for it as a *propaedeutic*,
or introductory instrument of general culture, has yet been
found.

In the seventeenth century John Locke (1632–1704)
voiced contemporary opinion when he wrote *à propos*
Logic,[1] " God has not been so sparing to men to make
them barely two-legged creatures, and left it to Aristotle
to make them rational." Locke expressly says that his
words were not meant " to lessen Aristotle ", and the
context shows that he did not intend them to ' lessen '
Logic. The words are not a gibe, but a serious reminder
that Logic ultimately owes its authority to nature and
nature's God; for behind our Logic, taught and self-
taught, there stands a Natural Logic, or (in Locke's
words) " a native faculty to perceive the coherence or
incoherence of its ideas ". Anyone who has taught Logic
with enjoyment and success builds on that Natural Logic
and appeals to that ' native faculty '; he does not attempt
to impart information from a dry textbook on a remote

[1] Locke's *Essay* IV, xvii 4.

subject; he awakens the logic that is dormant in the pupil's mind. And those who are teaching themselves Logic should act in the same spirit. Learning Logic is drudgery to those who merely memorize mechanical rules; the study takes on a new flavour and interest when viewed as a conscious awakening of an unconscious natural endowment. Let me add that the study acquires a new status and dignity when, with Locke, we view Natural Logic as a phase of our God-given reason, the pride and the privilege of man. The Greeks of old did not need Aristotle to teach them how to think and discourse rationally; no more do we; but they were the better thinkers and reasoners for his Logic, and so may we be. Aristotle would have been the last to wish us to bow to his *ipse dixit*, but only the ignorant or the narrow-minded will belittle our debt to him, and especially to his Logic.

What the study of Logic can do for you

Do not expect the wrong thing. Logic is no royal road. It will not teach you to know a good cigar; but it should help you to acquire and retain knowledge, and to detect a bad argument. Like drill and exercise Logic is an all-round tonic. Not only your thinking, but your speaking and writing should benefit; they should gain in clarity, precision, and firmness; the lack of Logic shows itself in the ' deficiency diseases ' of the mind— vagueness, woolliness of expression, and feeble grip of the matter in hand. ' All classes of books sold here.' It is not the classes, but the books that are sold. Why not tell the public so? It is just as easy, and more correct to say, ' Books of all classes sold here.' The study of Logic helps to correct such minor inaccuracies; logical analysis drills the mind into exactitude ; we learn to break up our sentences into their component parts ; we draw a circle, so to speak, round our subject, and another circle round our predicate ; and when we have drawn those two circles, then, and not till then, we know *precisely* what we are speaking about, and *precisely* what we are saying about it. Precision is the first fruit of the study of Logic, and precision will sharpen your statements, and add point and force to your arguments.

'My dear Sir, do be logical.' Almost certainly he is asking you to be consistent. Do not blow hot and cold about capital punishment, or whatever else is under discussion. Do not demand domestic economy and champagne suppers. Do not contradict yourself. Consistency in thought and speech, in feeling, character, and action, is a mark of rationality and a fruit of Logic.

Logic should help you in weighing *pros* and *cons*, and in sifting evidence ; the stage of logic-chopping and splitting hairs will soon pass, and will leave you with a mature, critical faculty and a standpoint of your own, Other disciplines can do this for you, too ; but Logic, where it acts, acts quickly.

Lastly, the study of Logic points beyond itself ; almost certainly it will introduce you to deep questions about mind and body, and to the problems of thought and thing. Such questions and problems are philosophical, and they lie outside the province of Logic proper ; but the thinker must meet them sooner or later, and the limits of Logic are not hard and fast ; at its lower levels Logic blends with grammar ; at its height Logic merges in philosophy.

Questions on Chapter I

1. What does Logic study? What are the practical aims of the discipline? What benefits may be expected from a course of Logic?

2. Why is it called *Formal* Logic?

3. What is formalism?

4. 'My dear Watson, the conclusion you draw about the case from your own observations is *valid*, but it is not *true*.' If you found that remark in Sherlock Holmes' *Memoirs*, what inference would you draw about his education? What would the remark mean?

5. What does Logic owe to Aristotle? Give an account of his life and writings? What was his *Organon*?

6. What is Natural Logic?

CHAPTER II

TERMS

DISCOURSE begins when something is ' proposed ', that is, set forth in terms, about something or someone. The Proposition is the unit of discourse, and the constituents of propositions are Terms. Propositions lead on to Inference. Connected Propositions yield syllogisms and other forms of inference. Terms, Propositions, and Syllogisms are the main elements of Aristotelian Formal Logic. We shall treat them in that order, but some anticipation here and there is unavoidable.

In a proposition of the simplest type there are two terms, the Subject and the Predicate. ' Silence is golden.' That is a proposition, believed by the speaker to be true, or at least proposed for acceptance in discourse as true. *Silence* is its Subject ; *golden* is its Predicate ; *golden* is predicated (affirmed) of *Silence*. The logical subject corresponds roughly to the grammatical subject ; it is that about which the statement is made. The logical predicate has no close equivalent in grammar ; but it has one sure mark ; it is that which is affirmed or denied about the subject. *Main* verbs (not verbs in relative clauses, etc.) belong to the predicate, and sometimes constitute it. The Copula (*is*, *are*, etc.) is discussed below (p. 34).

There are no terms, properly speaking, apart from propositions. The word *wolf* by itself, said or written, is not, strictly, a term ; it proposes nothing. In ' The wolf is coming ', *wolf* is a term. Of course, *wolf* by itself and other nouns and adjectives in isolation are often called terms, because they could be used as terms. Potentially they are terms ; they *could* be used as subject or predicate of a proposition, even when they are not actually being so used. Particles, prepositions, conjunctions, etc.—*the, a, in, of, but, when,* etc.—are not terms in the ordinary way. We cannot go far in discourse without them ; but we do not speak *of* them as a rule, nor predicate them of subjects.

A term may consist of one word, or of several words linked. Each of the following words or groups of words is one term, when subject or predicate of a proposition, or considered as such—wolf, big bad wolf, man, the human race, the sons of Adam, the daughters of Eve, ships that pass in the night, Shakespeare, the Swan of Avon, the last word of the finest sonnet of the Swan of Avon. A term *in its verbal aspect* is defined as, **A word or combination of words which can stand by itself as the subject or predicate of a proposition.**

But terms have another aspect which is expressed by, and is to some extent represented by, the word or combination of words. The real wolf bites ; the word *wolf* does not bite, though it expresses and to some extent represents the wolf that bites. A term *in its real aspect* is defined as, **Whatever we can think of and speak of as the subject or predicate of a proposition.**

This double meaning of the word *term* is accepted in life and sanctioned by usage, and we must accept it in Logic. It has its advantages and its disadvantages, and the former outweigh the latter. The context usually makes it quite clear which meaning is intended ; for instance, when we speak of Concrete Terms as persons or things, we are thinking and speaking of real terms. When we style *Socrates* a Concrete Term, we do not mean the eight-lettered name, Socrates, but the real Socrates who had a snub-nose and who drank the hemlock cheerfully. Some logicians try to get round the difficulty by distinguishing verbal terms as ‘names’ and real terms as ‘concepts’. This distinction eases the situation to some extent, but on the whole it raises more problems than it solves. It is better to keep the one word *term* with its two meanings, or two shades of meaning, and interpret it according to its context.

The word *term* comes from the Latin *terminus*, a limit or boundary; for the terms of a proposition limit the movement of the thought, as Euston and Paddington limit the movement of the trains.

The Order of the Terms

The order of the terms in a proposition is, for Logic, neither here nor there. In English we place the subject first, as a rule, and the predicate second. Aristotle in his Logic does the opposite. For emphasis we often reverse the order, as in ‘ Great is Diana of the Ephesians.’ *Great* comes first, but is not the subject; for nothing is said about it. *Diana of the Ephesians* comes second, but is not the predicate; for that goddess is the subject of the predication. The important thing to look at is, not the order of the terms, but the meaning of the proposition. About what (or whom) are we speaking? That is the first question to ask, and the answer to it gives the subject. The second question to ask is, What are we saying about the subject? The answer to it gives the predicate.

There are doubtful cases, like ‘ Honesty is the best policy ’. Is the subject *Honesty* or *The best policy*? It is arguable; for there are two possible propositions concealed, so to speak, in the proverb, and the context has to decide which of the two is intended. Generally, I think, people quote the proverb to answer the question, What is the best policy? How should I treat my customers? In that case *The best policy* is subject, and *honesty* is predicated of it. On the other hand, if a parent or teacher, wishing to commend honesty to the young, or if a moralist, discussing the sanctions of the moral law, quotes the same proverb, the words would have a different stress and would bear a different meaning. The parent or teacher or moralist would be taking *Honesty* as the subject, and would be predicating about it that it pays, that it is the best policy.

At this stage the student should practise himself in detecting terms, and in distinguishing subject and predicate. Take the following example of Mr. Jingle's narrative style (C. Dickens, *Pickwick Papers*, ch. 2). Imagine it is a telegram, just received, and that it is your job to translate it into ordinary prose for a newspaper column. With a little ingenuity you should be able to turn it into some twenty propositions, with forty terms, twenty subjects and twenty predicates.

Conquests! Thousands. Don Bolaro Fizzgig—Grandee—only daughter—Donna Christina—splendid creature—loved me to distraction—jealous father—high-souled daughter—handsome Englishman—Donna Christina in despair—prussic acid—stomach-pump in my portmanteau—operation performed—old Bolaro in ecstasies—consent to our union—join hands and floods of tears—romantic story—very.

Thought and Speech

Discourse is thought. Discourse is speech. Aristotle passes easily from thought to speech, and from speech to thought; and because the term 'discourse' covers and combines both activities, it is still the best general term for the subject-matter of logic. It keeps the student alive to the problem, but does not force upon him a rigid or premature solution. We meet the problems in various forms. How are terms related to words ? Terms are not the same as words ; but are they so very different ? How are judgments related to propositions ? How are inferences related to syllogisms ?[1] In all such questions the logician meets the one, wide, philosophical problem, How is thought related to speech ? The following remarks on the problem will indicate the position adopted in this book, and will, I hope, justify its phrasing, or the greater part of it.[2]

Thought and speech are very close to us, and it is hard to see them in perspective. They are clearly not the same thing ; yet they are not so very different. Sometimes we speak without thinking. Or do we ? Well, we speak quickly, without reflection, saying the first thing that comes into our heads, without ' stopping to think '. But we are thinking all the same. Sometimes, too, we think without speaking. Or do we ? Well, without audible speech, without speaking aloud ; but we may be speaking all the same. Inner speech is an inescapable fact. Is meditation thought or inner speech ? Who can say ? A speaker within makes a running commentary on the thinker's thoughts. We can often catch ourselves in the act of speaking to ourselves. In deep reflection, especially when men are under some emotional stress, lips move, tongue moves, vocal chords are a-quiver, framing retorts that are never said audibly, coining propositions that are never uttered.

---

[1] The term *syllogism* is explained below, p. 83.
[2] I add the qualification ; for I do not believe that absolute consistency is practicable or desirable.

In view of these facts it is unwise to identify the inner and the outer, or to press too far the distinction between them. In discourse the inner and the outer factors meet, but do not merge. The conventional view is that we first think and then express our thoughts in words; it is a useful convention up to a point; but applied to the finer points of Logic it misleads. It places speech in too subordinate a position, and blinds men to the wonder of words. Thought and speech are co-ordinate, concomitant functions of man's dual nature; because he is a rational spirit he thinks; because he is a rational spirit in a living body he utters ('outers') his thoughts, i.e. he speaks them. If we try to confine Logic to what goes on in the mind *or* to what goes on in the body we get into difficulties. Discourse is neither speechless thought, nor thoughtless speech. It is useless to make a clean cut between the judgment or concept in the mind and the proposition or term on the tongue. Speech is not a mere function of the body, like sneezing and coughing, and the union of speech with mind and spirit is an ultimate fact of our make-up which the logician must accept, as do other folk. His unit, the proposition, is a proposition *judged*, not merely spoken, and it is a proposition *uttered* (in speech or writing), not merely judged. A similar analysis applies to terms. Terms are words, but words conceived. Terms are concepts, but concepts uttered. Terms are words in a proposition; they are words *in* the mind of the speaker *for* the mind of the hearer. Words have their outer aspect; they can be heard when spoken, and seen when written down; but they have their inner aspect, too; they are far more than vibrations of air or spidery ink-marks on paper; words have meaning; they signify; and they thus have external reference, and can build up into creative constructions such as Shakespeare's plays.

The upshot for us is this : when you and I make a proposition, and set forth something in terms, we are not tying empty words or names together ; we are predicating something about someone or something, and we are saying what we believe to be true. For instance, when we say ' Man is mortal ', we are not saying that one name is another name ; we are not saying that the monosyllabic name *man* is the dissyllabic name *mortal* ; that would be untrue and nonsense ; we are affirming a judged fact about humanity, proposed and set forth in terms.

We come now to certain classifications of terms, important for the work of Logic.

Abstract and Concrete terms

In a *quiz* when people are trying to guess the object thought of, one of the first questions is, as a rule, Is it abstract ? If the answer is Yes, the mind goes off on generalities or qualities and objects which cannot be seen and touched. If the answer is No, we turn our attention to individual things, especially to visible and tangible things, to objects with definite shapes and sizes, and whose names do not end in -*ness*. We call the former class of objects Abstract, and the latter Concrete. It is only a rough and ready distinction, but it is a useful one in Logic and in life, provided we do not push it too far and are prepared for border-line cases. The working definition is as follows: *Concrete terms are persons or things ; Abstract terms are qualities or attributes of persons or things.*

The general notion behind the definition is that the mind starts with solid, compact objects, and reaches the less solid and less compact by a process of taking away or leaving out. By 'concrete reality' is usually meant the chair, the table, the stick, or the stone; for they and other sensible things are composed, so it appears, of clustered groups of qualities, of colours, touches, sounds, smells, and tastes, etc., that hang together like a swarm of bees, or like the grains of sand and drops of water and cement that compose builders' concrete. Sensible things present a firm front to the observer, and they are good instances of concrete reality; but they are not the only instances. Persons, composed of body and mind, of flesh and blood, of cells and tissue and fibres and nerves, of a myriad memories and thoughts, of hopes and fears and desires— persons also present a firm front to the observer, as we realize when a clash of personalities occurs.

To 'abstract' is to take away from, or to omit. The thief abstracts the notes from the wallet, and both from the pocket. Miss Dolly Daydreams is 'in a fit of abstraction' when her thoughts are far away. Abstraction is the mental act by which we detach, think apart, and remove from sight and attention those qualities, characteristics, aspects, and attributes which are in fact conjoined and given together in the concrete thing. There are two sides to any separation; if the notes are detached from the wallet, the wallet is detached from the notes. The name *abstract* is usually given to the part we take *into* our ken, but it can be given also to the part we leave outside. One of the aims and uses of abstraction is to find out what individuals or groups have in common, and so *abstract* often means the common element, as opposed to the individual feature, or the general as opposed to the particular.

In applying the distinction common sense must be

used. 'Humanity' is abstract, if it means the physical and moral qualities that make a man ; but in 'Humanity dreads war' it is equivalent to *mankind* or *all men*, and is therefore concrete.

Many abstract terms are not used in the plural, and not infrequently the -s, marking the plural, is an indication that a term, normally abstract, is being used *in concreto*, i.e. as concrete. In 'College society forms character', *society* is abstract ; in 'College societies run into debt', *societies* is concrete.

Singular, Common or General, and Collective terms

Singular terms are individuals, either persons, like *Socrates, Jack, Jill, the present chess champion, the 'reigning toast'*, or individual things, like *the Book of Kells, the first space-satellite, the last rose of summer, the largest fish in the lake.* Those designations which are permanently appropriated to an individual are called Proper Names. Singular terms are, as a rule, subjects of their propositions ; they can be predicated only of another Singular term ; e.g. 'The Principality is Wales', where the predicate tells what the subject designates.

Common terms are so called because they are *common* to several persons or things ; e.g. shoes, ships, sealing-wax, cabbages, kings. They are also called General terms, because they are shared by members of a *genus* or group. A Common term, when uniquely described, becomes Singular ; e.g. 'the gloomy Dean', 'the first Gentleman of Europe'.

Collective terms apply to groups of persons or things, but not to the individuals composing the group. Such are : the Parliament, the British Parliament, the militia, the South Down militia, the cricket club, the Marylebone Cricket Club.

Positive, Negative, Privative, Infinite, Contradictory, and Contrary terms

These are useful classifications, some for Logic, some for life, and some for both. The classes are not rigidly distinct; they are linked together, and there is some overlapping. They all turn on the fundamental difference between *Yes* and *No*. There are Yes-terms (terms of affirmation) and No-terms (terms of denial); and there are Yes-terms that shade off into No-terms, and there are No-terms that shade off into Yes-terms; for a *Yes* can suggest a *No*, and a *No* can suggest a *Yes*. Mere terms, that is terms outside judgments, neither affirm, deny, nor suggest; but we can speak of them as doing so because terms are viewed more properly as elements in judgments, which do affirm, deny, and suggest.

Positive terms are those that *posit*, i.e. affirm or suggest the presence of an attribute. Such are: gleaming, alive, true.

Negative terms are those that deny the presence of an attribute, or suggest its absence. Such are: dark, insincere, untrue.

Privative terms are those that deny the presence of an attribute, or suggest its absence, where its presence was to be expected. Such are: dumb, deaf, illogical.

The designations, *positive*, *negative*, and *privative* do not apply to all terms, but only to those that are attributes, and to the abstract terms that go with the attribute; e.g. happy, unhappy, happiness. Negative terms give rise to several *philosophical* difficulties that need not be discussed here. In Logic they are of importance in the rules of contradiction and contrariety (see below, p. 68), and in the processes of obversion and contraposition (see below, p. 74 ff.).

Infinite terms. A concrete, general term *negated*, like not-man, was called by Aristotle ' an infinite term '. Infinite terms are a class of contradictories, and in the logic of propositions they have an important place ; but viewed purely as terms, they have little significance. ' Beast is not man ' is a true and useful denial. ' Beast is not-man ' does not affirm anything significant about *Beast*. *Not-man* has been styled " a mere figment of logic " [1] ; as a term it has no meaning, and would not naturally occur to our thoughts. Why then is it called ' infinite ' ? Because if we suppose it to denote *everything that is not man*, there are no limits to its meaning. Fish, fowl, good red-herring, earth, air, fire, water, sun, moon, stars, and textbooks on logic—all that and much more is *not-man*, and is covered by the term. In this way of speaking *man* and *not-man* between them cover the universe, and leave nothing out. See below on the Law of the Excluded Middle (p. 125). The same holds of *worm* and *not-worm*, and any such pair of contradictories. It does not hold of pairs of attributive terms, like *hospitable* and *inhospitable*. *Inhospitable* has a meaning and occurs naturally in our thoughts. Whether it is to be classed as a negative term or privative is a matter of opinion, and depends on outlook ; but it is naturalized in language, as its form shows, and therein differs from *not-man*, and from terms like *non-consumer goods*, invented for purposes of contradiction and argument.

Contradictory and Contrary terms. Opposite pairs of terms are Contradictory or Contrary. Two terms are contra-

---

[1] H. W. B. Joseph, *An Introduction to Logic*, 2nd ed., p. 42.

dictory when the one is the negative of the other. Such are : white, not-white—wise, not-wise—late, not-late. The full significance of contradiction is best brought out by contrasting it with contrariety. Two terms are contrary when they are the most opposed of those coming under the one head or class. Such are : white, black— wise, foolish—late, early. *White* and *black* are usually regarded as colours, and (whether literally or metaphorically) as at opposite ends of the scale ; cf. " I am black, but O, my soul is white." [1] *Not-white* is far wider than *black* and goes outside the colour class (see above, p. 22, under *Infinite terms*). *Wise* and *foolish* apply only to intelligent beings ; *not-wise* can be applied as well to the inanimate ; *unwise* and *not-wise* are almost identical in meaning, when both are said of intelligent beings ; but *unwise* could not be said of the inanimate ; there is no difference between an *unwise* and a *not-wise* chess-player ; the automaton chess-player of last century could be called *not-wise*, but hardly *unwise*. Words like *unwise*, securely lodged in the language, tend to acquire a more positive meaning than their purely negative counterparts.

Contradictory terms are mutually exclusive ; they cannot both apply to the same thing ; if the one does not apply to a given thing, the other does. Contrary terms also are mutually exclusive ; the same object cannot be both wise and foolish ; but there are many objects that are neither wise nor foolish.

Connotation and Denotation. Intension and Extension

Common terms possess two distinct types of meaning, and the four technical terms in this section heading, or

[1] W. Blake, *The Little Black Boy.*

B

three of them at least, are required to make the distinction clear. We will take an instance.

What is a house? What does the term mean? What does it denote? Oh, it denotes anything from a city mansion to a shooting lodge. A cottage is a house; so is a suburban villa, and so is a royal palace. The term *house* means those buildings, and many more. You could point to any of those buildings, and say, That is a *house*. The term *house* denotes all those buildings. That type of meaning is called Denotation, and that cottage, palace, villa, lodge, etc., are all part of the denotation of the term *house*.

Thank you for the information, says Mr. Jones, your friend in the Civil Service; but it is not what I want. Pointing at buildings does not help *me*; for I am Chairman of a Housing Committee; we are drafting a Housing Bill; we need to know what a house *is*, what constitutes a house, what the term *house* essentially means, or shall mean for purposes of the Act. We want to know what *house* connotes, or shall for our present purpose connote.

This deeper meaning is called Connotation.[1] It is harder to come at than denotation in most cases; anyone can point to a building and recognize it as a house; but not everyone is prepared to say precisely what constitutes a house. Connotation is a statement of the essential attributes of the term, and such a statement is often a matter for experts. The essential attributes of a house would include at any rate, (1) building or structure, to exclude caves, etc., (2) permanence, to exclude tents, booths, caravans, etc., (3) fitness for human habitation, to exclude sheds, sties, etc. On the basis of such a list

[1] From the Latin *connotare*, used by the Scholastics to express the notion of a second, or supplemental, meaning.

the connotation of the term *house* would be, ' a permanent building fit for human habitation '. Housing Acts would almost certainly require more precise attributes, such as some upper and lower limits of size in terms of floor-space.

All common terms carry this twofold meaning. I suggest that the reader should choose one or two with which he is familiar, say, table, boat, or car, and work out for himself in detail the connotation and denotation of each ; when he is clear on the difference, let him tackle with me the further distinction between Intension and Extension.

Intension is quite easy. It is what you intend your term to mean. It is the inner meaning, given to the term by the public, the expert, or yourself. It is a statement of the attributes, and is therefore identical with connotation, and the two technical terms for the one thing are not really needed. In some ways intension is the better term, but on balance connotation is to be preferred, because it has the cognate verb *to connote*. We can say that the term *house connotes* so and so, but not that it *intends* so and so.[1]

Extension is used by some logicians as the equivalent of Denotation ; but it is better to keep the names distinct, and there is work for both of them to do. They are alike in facing outwards ; in *that* both are opposed to both connotation and intension ; but while denotation points the finger at the individual, extension waves the hand towards the class to which the individual belongs. The term *boat* extends to and covers the classes of rowing-boat, fishing smack, yacht, barge, liner, battleship, etc. Those

---

[1] Some logicians distinguish the two terms, making Connotation relatively fixed and objective, and Intension varying with the individual. The distinction is hard to sustain.

classes are part of the extension of the term. But if we
descend from the classes to the individual boats, then we
must speak of denotation. The term *boat* denotes Noah's
Ark, the flagship of Solomon's navy, the fastest trireme
that fought at Salamis, the *Golden Hind*, Nelson's *Victory*,
the *Queen Mary*, the Kish lightship in Dublin Bay, and
millions more.

Inverse Variation of Connotation and Extension

Very often when we increase the connotation of a term
we automatically decrease its extension, and, *vice versa*,
when we decrease its connotation, we increase its extension.
A boat is a structure that floats on water; add *wooden* to
the connotation, and the number of classes in the extension
is reduced. On the other hand omit *structure*, and the
number of classes is increased; for rafts, hollow logs and
planks might rank as boats.

Practice in varying connotation and extension and
observing the results is of use in classifying, and in fixing
definitions. Whether the variation is inverse in all cases
may be doubted (see Joseph, *op. cit.*, p. 137 ff.). Note
also that what goes for extension does not always go for
denotation. You can alter the number of trout in the lake
without altering the number of classes of trout; but it
would be hard to alter the number of their classes without
altering the number of trout. If you alter the connotation
of a term, almost certainly you alter its denotation; but
alter its denotation without altering its extension, and you
do not alter its connotation.

Non-connotative terms[1]

J. S. Mill taught that proper names and specific abstract terms have no connotation. In his eyes *Sir Walter Scott*, for instance, has only one meaning; it would denote the famous writer of that name, but *connote* nothing, not even a person of the male sex or the author of *Waverley*. On this view his name is a mark distinguishing him from other people, but otherwise without meaning. His name may suggest his sex and what he was and did, but does not mean any of those things.

Bosanquet[2] thought that Mill was wrong on the point, and said that a proper name " has a connotation, but not a fixed general connotation "; but whether a private and personal connotation, particularly if always changing, could come up to what we ordinarily mean by ' connotation ' seems very doubtful. Connotation is usually taken to imply common attributes of a relatively fixed character; and provided we distinguish *acquired* meaning from original, and limit Mill's doctrine to a denial of original meaning in proper names it is correct. (As to abstract terms Mill is on weaker ground.) Many proper names, such as Smith, were not originally proper names, but common terms, and of course *then* they had a connotation; but that fact does not affect the present question.

Definition

Definition is a difficult art, but a necessary duty in honest discourse, especially when unfamiliar or ambiguous terms

---

[1] The question is of minor importance. Those who wish to pursue it should read J. S. Mill, *Logic* I ii 5, and, for different views, H. W. B. Joseph, op. cit., p. 150 ff. (2nd ed.).

[2] B. Bosanquet, *The Essentials of Logic*, Lect. V.

have to be employed. Unless we define our terms with such degree of accuracy as the subject-matter and our knowledge permit, clear thought and convincing statement are impossible. To *define* a term is to state its limits (*fines*). Connotation gives the limits, and therefore *Definition is the statement of the connotation of the term.*

The perfect definition is an ideal; but some are better than others. Faulty and weak definitions, and even mere descriptions (see below, p. 30), can be better than nothing. To make weak definitions stronger, and bad ones better, and to set a high standard for all who define, the following five *Rules of Definition* have long been laid down. The fifth Rule carries with it most of the requirements of the other four.

(1) The definition must be *Adequate*, i.e. *Commensurate*; it must measure up to the term to be defined; it must fit like a glove, and be neither too wide nor too narrow. The extension and denotation of the term test the adequacy of the definition. The definition is adequate if the classes and individuals it covers are exactly equal to those covered by the term defined, and are neither too many, nor too few. Examples:

(*a*) 'A gillaroo[1] is a trout with a gizzard.' The definition is adequate. The number of trouts with a gizzard, and of their classes, is exactly equal to the number of gillaroos and of their classes.

(*b*) 'A musical comedy is a dramatic representation with a happy ending.' The definition is too wide; it covers all comedies.

(*c*) 'A University student is a man on the books of

[1] The word 'gillaroo' comes from the Irish 'giolla ruadh', and means 'red fellow'. The species is found in some Irish lakes, notably Lough Mask. Whether its 'gizzard' is a true gizzard is, in its turn, a question of definition.

a University.' The definition is too narrow; most universities today admit women.

(2) The definition must be *Precise* and *Clear*. It must not contain anything superfluous, nor be expressed in obscure or ambiguous terms. Examples:

(a) ' An isosceles triangle is a three-sided rectilinear figure with two of its sides equal.' The definition is precise and clear.

(b) ' An isosceles triangle is a three-sided rectilinear figure with two of its sides equal and its three angles together equal to two right angles.' The definition is not precise; it needs pruning; the latter clause is superfluous.

(3) The definition must not contain a term equivalent to the term to be defined. A breach of this rule is called, *A Circle in Definition*. Circular definitions go round on themselves, and make no advance. Examples:

(a) " Network—Any thing reticulated or decussated, at equal distances, with interstices between the intersections " (Dr. S. Johnson). Circular (*rete* is Latin for a *net*) and contains something superfluous.

(b) And what *is* an archdeacon ? ' An archdeacon, my dear Sir, is a man who performs archidiaconal functions.' Circular.

(c) ' Life is the operation of vital forces.' Circular; *vita* is Latin for *life*.

(4) As far as possible the definition should not be by negative attributes. Examples:

(a) ' Matter is something we know not what.' Though partly positive in form, the nerve of the definition relates to ignorance, i.e. not-knowing.

(b) ' A teetotaller is one who does not drink alcoholic beverages.' ' Teetotaller' is a privative term, and it is hardly possible to define it in fully positive terms.

(5) The definition should be *per genus et differentiam*.
A *genus* (see below, p. 131) is a group or family, especially
a natural family or kind. A *differentia* is that which distinguishes one species in a *genus* from another species.
Trout is a *genus*. Gillaroo trout have a lump in the throat
that grinds down the shells of water-snails ; and that lump
is the *differentia* of the gillaroo species of trout. The
definition given above under (1) (*a*) is therefore *per genus
et differentiam*. Here is another instance : *Homo animal
risibile*, i.e. Man is an animal that can laugh. ' Man is an
animal ', that is true, but it is no definition ; for it leaves
man undefined in a wide ocean of other animals. ' Man
can laugh ', that is true, and a most significant truth,
implying conscious self-reference ; but it is no definition ;
it does not pin-point *man* ; only when we put the two
truths together, do we reach a worthy definition at the
point of intersection. We must first compare ourselves
with the other animals in the *genus* that, like ourselves,
live, breathe, and move, and then contrast ourselves with
those that cannot laugh, and have not our *differentia*.
When we have thus considered the term *man per genus*,
and then *per differentiam*, we have determined its ' bound-
aries ' (*fines*) ; we have *defined man*, and, incidentally, can
appreciate the gift of laughter.

Description

Description is a partial statement of the connotation of
the term, sufficient to distinguish it from other terms. To
the logician, a description is an imperfect definition, but
to the man of letters description is a fine art and a difficult
art. Individuals can be described, but not, strictly, defined.
' A gillaroo is a fish '—that description goes a very short

way; but it might be better than nothing. 'A gillaroo is a trout'—that is better again. 'Pleasure is a test of a formed habit'—that is a good Aristotelian description, not far from a definition.

Division

Logical Division is like analysis in the experimental sciences; it breaks up the material into its component parts. Division is the complementary process to definition, dealing with extension and denotation, as definition deals with connotation. Division is much like Classification; but in Division we start with the whole and work down to the parts, while in Classification we usually start with the parts and work up to the whole. For instance, a treatise on the racial characters of man would have to begin by dividing mankind into Aryans, Semites, Magyars, etc. The main divisions would be sub-divided, and the sub-divisions perhaps sub-divided. The resulting table could be called 'a Division of Man', or 'a Classification of men'. Division is mainly concerned with the orderly arrangement of class and species; but class and species can be divided into the individuals composing them. Individuals themselves are not capable of logical division; hence their name.

There are three main Rules of Logical Division:

(1) It must be *adequate*. The parts must together be equal to the whole, and no part must be overlooked. Example:

The contents of Logic are divided into terms, propositions, and syllogisms. In dividing natural species, etc., it is often hard to ensure that no part has been omitted.

(2) It must be *distinct*. There must be no overlapping

or blurred outlines. Europeans are correctly divided into British, Irish, French, Germans, Dutch, Swedish, etc., but not into British, Scottish, Irish, French, Germans, Dutch, Swedish, Scandinavians, etc. The logic of the shop-sign ' Ladies, Gents, and Clerical Tailoring ' is open to criticism.

(3) *There must be only one Principle of Division.* The Principle of Division is the basis on which the division is made. If we divide mankind by race or by colour, then race or colour is the Principle of Division. Whatever Principle we adopt, we must stick to it, as far as possible. We must not divide mankind into Aryans, Semites, white men, redskins, intellectuals, workers, ancients, and moderns. Books may be divided into fiction, history, travel, poetry, biography, etc., but not into fiction, octavo, quarto, manuscript, printed, bound and unbound. It is not always possible or desirable to keep strictly to this rule ; and if the two Principles are very close or congruous, a cross-division will do no great harm.

Dichotomy

Dichotomy is a form of division, suggested by Plato and criticized by Aristotle. The word means ' cutting into two parts '. Dichotomy divides a *genus* into two parts, one of which possesses the *differentia* and the other *not*. Thus *animal* would dichotomize into rational and irrational. Rational beings would dichotomize into mortal and immortal. The division is necessarily exhaustive, and the species necessarily exclude one another. The method is of some use, and we still divide into vertebrates and invertebrates; but the members of the class *invertebrates* have, most of them, little in common. The historic dichotomy, known as *Arbor Porphyriana*, is shown below (p. 134).

Questions and Exercises on Chapter II

1. Define *term* as used in Logic. Give its derivation. How does a *term* differ from a *word*?

2. How do we know the difference between Subject and Predicate? Which comes first?

3. The problem of thought and speech meets us everywhere in Logic. A final solution must obviously wait on experience and mature reflection. Can you suggest a commonsense approach to the problem in the early stages of Logic?

4. Take a paragraph or two from the news columns of a daily paper. List the nouns that could serve as *terms*; then classify them as abstract, concrete, or doubtful. Discuss the doubtful cases.

5. Arrange the following terms under the headings, Singular, Common, Collective: The Queen of Sheba, Solomon's navy, the Light Brigade, the Charge of the Light Brigade, the first breath of spring, bee, the queen bee, queen bees, Jacob, ladder, Jacob's Ladder, European, John Smith, Smith and Co. Ltd.

6. What difficulties are associated with negative terms? How do negative terms differ from privative?

7. Does 'not-man' mean anything? What did Aristotle call it? Why?

8. Give the contradictories of the following: A, kindly, book, logical, warm, foolish.

9. Give the contraries of the following: Alpha, man, warm, foolish.

10. Why are several technical terms needed for *meaning* in logic?

11. Give the connotation and denotation of the terms, motor-car, party.

12. Explain 'the inverse variation of connotation and extension'. Discuss it.

13. Do proper names connote anything?

14. Give with examples the rules of definition and division.

15. 'I could describe a Regatta; but I could not define the term.' Comment.

16. Discuss the value of dichotomy.

CHAPTER III

PROPOSITIONS

THE structure of the Proposition was outlined in the previous chapter; for terms cannot be understood apart from propositions. Propositions are as necessary to terms as terms are to propositions. In this chapter we discuss the Proposition in detail. We first deal with those comparatively simple propositions, like 'Silence is golden', which are called Categorical; they assert *categorically*, that is, without conditions or strings. We then (from p. 56) discuss non-Categorical propositions.

Propositions in the Logic of discourse 'propose' something about something or someone; they 'propose' a predicate about a subject; they affirm a predicate of a subject, or they deny a predicate of a subject. Each such proposition has therefore two terms, a subject and a predicate, not isolated but joined by the copula, expressed or implied. *The subject is that about which the affirmation or denial is made. The predicate is that which is affirmed or denied of the subject.* In 'Silence is golden' *Silence* is subject, *golden* is predicate, and *is* is copula.

The Copula

The Copula is the hinge of the proposition; on it turns the relation between subject and predicate. The copula is the connecting link. Silence is silence, and golden is golden; but if you wish to express the golden character of silence, you must connect the two words by the copula.

No copula, expressed or implied, no proposition. Take away the copula (e.g. 'silence, golden'), and the unity of the proposition is destroyed, and its two terms fall asunder, like a broken coupling.

The copula, if expressed, is the present tense of the verb *to be*—is, is not, are, are not, etc. If the copula is expressed, the predicate is often an adjective or an adjectival attribute. Examples:

Larch trees are deciduous.

Fir trees are not deciduous.

The elephant is long-lived.

The mouse is not long-lived.

Cycling is the cheapest form of transport.

Books are a solace to the weary.

A policeman's lot is not a happy one.

The copula, if implied, is shown usually by the inflection of the verb. Examples:

Birds fly.

Ostriches cannot fly.

Sunshine ripens the corn.

The moon does not affect the weather.

Starlings congregate in the autumn.

History repeats itself.

Traffic-lights facilitate the traffic.

Statesmen must compromise.

In poetry the copula can be left entirely to the imagination. Examples:

Happy the man who all his time and toil
Hath spent through life upon his native soil! (i.e. Happy *is* the man who . . .)

Felix qui potuit rerum cognoscere causas. (i.e. Felix *est* qui . . .)

The copula is a mark of predication; it shows that something is asserted or denied of a subject. It is not a mark of existence. When we say 'The elephant is long-lived', we do not say, or mean, that the elephant exists long-lived. Existence may be implied; but what we affirm is simply that the attribute *long-lived* applies to the species *elephant*. The notion of *existence* comes in, not from the copula, but from the fact that we usually speak about *existent* things.[1]

The copula does not indicate present time. In 'Socrates is mortal' nothing is said about the present existence of Socrates; when we say it, we are scarcely thinking of time at all, and any latent time-reference there may be in the proposition as a whole is certainly not expressed by the copula. How to deal with propositions that make explicit assertions about past, present, or future time is shown below (p. 42).

Propositions and Sentences

Our propositions come from the limitless sea of human discourse. They are sentences to which the principles of Logic apply; they are selected in accordance with those principles, and are 'prepared', to meet the requirements of logical form. In other words, we select our propositions from the raw material of sentences, and then 'prepare' them and fit them for the processes of Logic.

All propositions are sentences, but not all sentences are propositions. Ejaculations, exclamations, prayers, wishes, commands, and questions are not propositions. The distinguishing mark of a proposition is its capacity for truth or falsity. A sentence is a proposition for Logic if, and only if, it is capable of being true or false. The one sentence cannot be true *and* false at the same time; but to

---

[1] The various meanings of *existence* form a philosophical problem. It and the implications as to the existence of subject and predicate in the different types of propositions are usually discussed in more advanced works on Logic under the heading, 'Existential Import'.

take its place in Logic and to rank as a proposition, it
must be of such a character that we can say of it, ' That is
true ' or ' That is false.' ' How many miles to Babylon ? '
' Turn again, Whittington.' ' Wasn't that a pretty dish
to set before a king ! ' ' May I die the death of the
righteous.'—Such sentences are not capable of being true
or false. They are not propositions. ' Whittington was
Lord Mayor of London.' ' The birds began to sing.'
' He died the death of the righteous.'—Such sentences are
capable of being true or false ; they are propositions.

In applying this rule, go by the sense, and not by the
sound or the look. There are sentences that do not look
like propositions, but *are*, and there are sentences that look
like propositions, but are *not*. " Are not Abana and
Pharpar, rivers of Damascus, better than all the waters of
Israel ? " [1] That is a *rhetorical* question ; one does not
answer it ; for it is the same as saying, ' Abana and
Pharpar . . . are better than all the waters of Israel.' It
can be true ; it can be false ; it is a proposition. ' Horatius kept the bridge '—that is true ; it is a proposition.
' Lars Porsena kept the bridge '—that is false ; it is a
proposition. ' Who will stand on either hand, and keep
the bridge with me ? '—that is a question ; it cannot be
true or false ; it is not a proposition. ' Herminius will
stand at my right hand, and keep the bridge with me ? '—
that, too, is a question, though it looks like a proposition ;
we know it by the question mark ; Herminius knew it by
the tone of voice and rising inflection. Horatius' prayer
to Father Tiber, his wishes and vows, his orders (if any)
to his comrades—such sentences lie outside the scope of
Logic ; they are not propositions ; they cannot be true
or false.

[1] 2 Kings v 12.

'Preparing' the Proposition

The Proposition must be 'prepared' for the technical processes of Logic, as specimens in the laboratory are 'prepared' for the microscope. Not all propositions are equally suitable for logical treatment at the elementary stages, and of those that are suitable some are the better of minor alterations in form. Logic, like other disciplines, has its natural limits, and cannot deal efficiently with all propositions. Those on the following list and others like them are unsuitable for logical treatment. They are propositions; they admit truth or falsity; but in one respect or another they fail to measure up to the standards of subject-predicate form:

> It is snowing.
> It never rains, but it pours.
> Anything might happen.
> There is nothing there.
> He is not here.
> A is equal to B.
> This is greater than that.
> Boys will be boys.
> There's many a slip 'twixt cup and lip.
> The expedition is one hundred miles from the South
>   Pole.

It is just a list of types of proposition; it could be expanded indefinitely, and could be criticized both for what it contains and for what it omits. It is meant to cover, (*a*) colloquialisms, like 'Boys will be boys', which is little more than an exclamation or grunt, (*b*) vague and conventional statements about common physical phenomena, where we do not know precisely what is what, or what does what, (*c*) statements of abstract relations, such as mathematical equality or comparative size, and (*d*) statements of position, distance, and other spatial relations. They have all one thing in common ; they are deficient in respect of subject-predicate form. Either the terms are unclear, or the predication is vague ; either we cannot say precisely what the subject is, or what the predicate is, or what exactly is affirmed or denied. Such propositions lack therefore requirements of ' logical form ', and we can afford to ignore them. It is not the duty of Logic to deal with every type of proposition, every type of sentence, every nicety of discourse. Logic has better and more important material, and can never run short of clear affirmations and denials about sterling subjects of worth-while knowledge. Logic gains, not loses, if types of propositions, unsuitable for logical treatment, are left aside.

Setting out the Proposition in Logical Form

By ' Logical Form ' I mean the most convenient form for teaching Logic, Aristotelian Logic. There is room for difference of opinion about the phrase ' Logical Form ', and from one point of view any subject-predicate proposition is *eo ipso* in logical form. Anyone is entitled to take up that position, and whoever does so has only to regard the following instructions as explaining how to set out the proposition in *fuller* or *optimum* logical form.

There are two distinct steps to be taken, and the two rules for taking them are : (1) Express the *quantity* of the proposition, if it is not expressed already, and (2) Express the copula, if it is not expressed already, and make consequential changes in the predicate. We will explain and illustrate both these rules.

(1) Take our proposition, 'Silence is golden.' It is capable of truth or falsity. Its subject and its predicate are both perfectly clear ; its predication is well defined. It has passed the initial tests, and might appear to be in full logical form. But is it ? No. We should find it defective, if we tried to use it in argument ; for we have not yet been told whether *golden* is said of *all* silence, or only of *some*. Silence, where we ought to speak, can be anything but golden ; it can even be brazen. This defect in Logic must, if possible, be put right. The Quantity of the proposition and the Distribution of its subject (which amount to the same thing, see below, p. 49) are to be expressed, if that is not already done, and if we have the material for doing so. By this 'grooming', if we may call it so, the pair of indefinite propositions, symbolized by 'A is B' and 'A is not B' becomes the quartet of definite propositions, on which the primary work of Logic centres, viz.

> All A is B.
> No A is B.
> Some A is B.
> Some A is not B.

(2) The second step concerns the copula. Take the proposition, 'Silence gives consent.' Strictly its logical form is just as good as the logical form of (say) 'Silence is golden.' Subject, predicate, and predication are perfectly clear in both cases. The one states what silence *is*, the other what silence *does*. The word *consenting* is not used absolutely ; if it were, 'Silence is consenting' could be substituted for 'Silence gives consent', just as 'Sea trout are migrants' can be substituted for 'Sea trout migrate.' We must, however, recognize that syllogistic

and other processes in Aristotelian Logic are, as a rule, more conveniently and with less risk of error, carried out with propositions that express the copula and have adjectival predicates or the equivalent. Whether this is due to an accident of language or to some deeper reason, we need not here discuss. Aristotle recognized ' Man walks ' as a good logical proposition ; but the vast majority of the examples in his Organon are of the ' A is B ' type. We follow his example. Without any reflection on the logical character of propositions that only *imply* the copula, we shall regard those that *express* the copula, as being for practical purposes of Logic in *optimum* logical form, and shall ' set out ' the proposition accordingly, wherever language permits and it can conveniently be done.

Exercises in logical form. Practical instructions

Make a list of propositions of your own choosing, and work them out on paper. Choose easy examples at first, and vary the type. Avoid long, complex, and highly idiomatic propositions. Make sure that all *are* propositions, i.e. are capable of truth or falsity. Admit only those with a clearly marked subject and predicate. Include both affirmations and denials. Include both those with the copula expressed and those with the copula implied.

Have three columns, one for the Subject, one for the Copula, and one for the Predicate. Under subject and predicate, respectively, enter the whole term not the noun only, but also its adjective, relative clause, and anything that logically goes along with it. Enter the negative (if any) with the copula in the rough work. When the mark of quantity is added in the fair copy, the ' all ' of a universal negative combines with the ' not ' to make ' No ' which is prefixed to the proposition. On no account allow such propositions to keep the form ' All . . . not ' (see below, p. 54). If the mark of quantity (*all* or *some*) is not expressed, and if you can tell which is intended, add it.

Then tackle those propositions that need to have the copula expressed, with consequential changes in the predicate. Your aim should be to convey the same sense with the minimum of outward change ; that usually means transferring the idea of the verb into an adjective or adjectival clause, and making it the predicate or part of it. Since the copula does not express the notion of time, propositions, like ' Babylon was once a great city ', or ' Troy will rise from its ruins ' must be treated in one or other of two ways. (*a*) Transfer the time-notion to the predicate, and write ' Babylon is what was once a great city ', and ' Troy is a fortress that will rise from its ruins ', or (*b*) Ignore the time-notion, and write simply, ' Babylon is a great city ', and ' Troy rises from its ruins.' The former method is usually clumsy, and the latter method is usually both neat and adequate. What we are really doing when we ignore the time-notion is just what poets, historians, and *raconteurs* do in vivid narrative ; we are picturing ourselves as contemporary with the events of which we speak ; we are projecting our thoughts backwards or forwards into (what might be called) ' the timeless present of logical predication '.

Finally, do not waste time on stubborn propositions. The resources of language are limited, and if you cannot find a good adjectival or attributive equivalent for your verb, turn to some other proposition. Examples :

Propositions	*In logical form*
Men die.	All men are mortal.
Cain killed Abel.	Cain is the killer of Abel.
Grass is green.	All grass is green.
Water does not run uphill.	No water runs uphill.
Abel was killed by Cain.	Abel is the man who was killed by Cain.
Feathered animals have bills.	All feathered animals have bills.
Learning satisfies the learned.	Learning is a satisfaction to the learned.
All leaves taper to a point.	All leaves are pointed.
No sugars are insoluble in water.	(the same)
No birds have four legs.	No birds are quadrupeds.
' The quality of mercy is not strained.'	No acts of mercy are of strained quality.
Poachers do not observe the law.	No poachers are law-abiding.
Rolling stones gather no moss.	No rolling stones are mossy (or, discarding the metaphor), None who change jobs frequently are successful.
Virtuous people do not always succeed in life.	Some virtuous people are not successful.
It is a wise father who knows his own child.	All fathers who know their own children are wise.
Virtue alone is happiness below.	All who are happy on earth are virtuous.
Steam is H_2O.	All steam is H_2O.

Propositions and Symbols

From this on considerable use will be made of symbols both for terms and for propositions.   S is the accepted

symbol for the subject, and P for the predicate. ' S is P '
is the accepted symbol for the affirmative proposition,
and ' S is not P ' for the negative. SP can be used where
there is no need to distinguish affirmative from negative.
Other symbols will be introduced, and mentioned, as the
need for them arises.

Symbols have their uses and their abuses. They are
a mental shorthand, enabling much ground to be covered
in a short time; further, they encourage the mind to
attend to propositional form without being distracted by
colourful content. But the use of symbols in Logic is
not an end in itself; too many symbols at an early stage
make the study of Logic much harder than it need be.
In the following pages the rules of Logic are illustrated,
so far as is practicable, both in abstract symbols and in
concrete terms. The student is recommended to do his
practice work along similar lines, at least until his mind
turns with ease from the concrete case to the abstract
symbol, and back again from the abstract symbol to the
concrete case.

The Quality of Propositions

Quality is a specialized term in Logic; the word comes
from the Latin *qualis*, which means, Of what sort? Of
what sort is the proposition? What is its fundamental
character? Is it affirmative or is it negative? Propositions have either the affirmative quality or the negative
quality. They are either affirmations or denials. There
are several ways of expressing denials in English. The
two chief forms are :

S is not P.
No S is P.

Equipollent Propositions

Propositions that differ in quality, but have the same meaning, the same subject, and contradictory predicates, are called Equipollent. Such are:

> Conversation is a pleasant pastime.
> Conversation is not an unpleasant pastime.

Affirmation is one thing; denial is another thing; and the same proposition cannot both affirm and deny. How then is Equipollence possible? Because when the proposition is taken as a whole an alteration in the quality of the predication can be offset by an equal and opposite alteration in the predicate. Equipollent propositions, understood as they occur in living discourse, generally display slight differences of tone or emphasis.

The machinery of Equipollence is as follows: If the given proposition is negative, the negation is simply transferred from the predication or the copula to the predicate. 'S is not P' becomes 'S is not-P'. If the given proposition is affirmative, two negations are introduced, one into the predication or copula, the other into the predicate, thus cancelling out. 'S is P' becomes 'S is not not-P'. The change operates more smoothly when the copula is expressed and the predicate is adjectival; and for the purpose of Equipollence the proposition, if not already in this form, should be put into it.

As a process of Inference Equipollence is called Obversion (see below, p. 74), and is of technical importance on that account. In actual discourse it is used to alter the tone of statements. A Chairman might not like to call an item of business 'important', but might prefer to say it was 'not unimportant'.

The Quantity of Propositions and of their Terms

The Quantity (Latin, *quantum*) of a proposition is the answer to the question, How much does it affirm or deny ? What is the extent of its assertion ? The Quantity of its Terms is the answer to similar questions about its subject and its predicate.

The proposition is a statement about its subject, and therefore the extent and reference of the proposition and of its subject are necessarily the same. If the subject is ' All men ', the proposition is about ' All men '; if the subject is ' Some men ', the proposition is about ' Some men '. *The quantity of the proposition is the same as that of its subject.* The Quantity of the Predicate is a different matter, and is determined in a different way, and, as a rule, is not called Quantity, but is called Distribution instead. The Quantity of the subject, too, is better known as Distribution. We speak, therefore, of the *Quantity* of the proposition, and of the *Distribution* of its Terms.

In respect of Quantity three classes of propositions are recognized by Logic, viz. Universal, Particular, and Singular. Universal propositions are about the whole of a kind. Examples :

> All woodcock have long bills.
> Snipe (*sc.* all snipe) have long bills.
> No partridge have long bills.

Particular propositions are about part of a kind. Examples :

> Some duck dive.
> Weather forecasts can be accurate.
> Some pheasants do not crow.

Singular propositions are about an individual person or thing. Examples :

> Noah built an ark.
> The first animal to enter was the last to leave.
> The earliest primrose is not the best.

Singular propositions, for most purposes, can be treated, and are treated, as universal ; for their subjects, being singular, are necessarily taken in their whole extent. ' Some Socrates ' makes no sense. In the main, then, we have only to think of two quantities in Logic, universal and particular.

Logical Quantity is not concerned with numbers. When we say " All men are mortal ", we are not thinking of millions or billions of men, or of any aggregate of men. Races, nations, classes, families, and individuals are covered by the assertion ; but the assertion itself is not about any count of men, but about that without which there would be no men to count, viz. the human kind, humanity, Man. *All* in logic means the whole kind ; *Some* in logic means part of the kind, at least one ; the words *All* and *Some* give no further indication as to numbers.

Quality and Quantity taken together

There are two types of proposition according to Quality, affirmative and negative, and there are two types (for our purpose) according to Quantity, universal and particular. Thus there are four types in all, universal affirmative, universal negative, particular affirmative, and particular negative. To each of these four types of proposition a symbolic vowel, as shown in the following table, has been assigned. A and I stand for the two affirmative types ;

E and O for the two negative types. They are easy to remember ; for A and I are the first two vowels of *affirmo*, I affirm, and E and O are the vowels of *nego*, I deny.

THE FOUR TYPES OF PROPOSITION[1]

A	Universal Affirmative	.	.	All S is P	S a P
E	Universal Negative	.	.	No S is P	S e P
I	Particular Affirmative	.	.	Some S is P	S i P
O	Particular Negative	.	.	Some S is not P	S o P

Singular Propositions

Singular propositions have a singular term for subject. Examples:

> Socrates taught Plato.
> Socrates did not teach Aristotle.

As stated above they rank as universals for most purposes (A or E). Some logicians place them in a class apart, neither universal nor particular. On balance the present arrangement is to be preferred. Four types are easier to manage than six, and singular propositions *are* like universal propositions in that their subjects are wholes, not aggregates.

Enumerative Propositions

Enumerative Propositions are those that gather together a limited number of instances of a class or members of a kind, and enumerate them in one statement, usually prefaced by ' All the . . .' or ' All these . . .' They have to

[1] The student may use the shorthand notation of the fourth column when he is thoroughly familiar with the rules of Inference ; till then he should use the notation in the third column.

be treated as universals in Logic, but they fall short of true universality in respect of their extension and denotation. For example, ' All the Apostles were Jews ' is an Enumerative proposition ; it enumerates and summarizes a set of given instances. St. Peter was a Jew. St. James, St. John, etc. were Jews. Therefore all these Apostles, *mentioned*, were Jews. Compare it with a true universal, like ' All Apostles have a sense of mission ', and one sees the difference at a glance. The former proposition is based on a limited list of individuals, the latter proposition is based on the notion and meaning of apostleship.

The Distribution of Terms in a Proposition

A term is said to be Distributed if the whole of it is covered by the predication ; and if only part of it is covered by the predication, it is said to be Undistributed. In ' All lunar eclipses occur at the full-moon ' *lunar eclipses* is Distributed ; for there are none not covered by the statement ; but *occur at the full-moon* is Undistributed ; for there are many other occurrences at that time. *Distributed* and *Undistributed*, said of terms, correspond, respectively, to *Universal* and *Particular*, said of propositions ; some logicians use *Universal* and *Particular* quantitatively of terms as well as of propositions.

The Distribution of the subject, as already explained (p. 46), goes along with the quantity of the proposition. If the proposition is Universal, affirmative or negative (A or E), the subject is Distributed, and if the subject is Distributed, the proposition is Universal. If the proposition is Particular, affirmative or negative (I or O), the subject is Undistributed, and if the subject is Undistributed, the proposition is Particular.

In deciding the quantity of the proposition and the distribution of the subject, go by the sense. Many universals have no outward mark of quantity. Most proverbs, just because they are proverbs, are universal. General statements, like ' Roses suffer from green-fly ' are usually intended universally. On the other hand, ' All ' prefixed is no guarantee of universality. On the enumerative ' All ' see above (p. 48), and on the idiomatic ' All . . . not ' see below (p. 54).

Questions about Quantity concentrate attention on extension and denotation, and tend to make us forget that terms have connotation as well. Individuals form groups in virtue of connotation shared. Some swans are white, and some swans are black, and those that are white are not those that are black ; but all swans share ' swanship ', which is a deeper and broader thing than surface colour. ' Swanship ' means the connotation of the term *swan*, its essential attributes, and in virtue of it the two propositions, ' Some swans are white, and some black ' have the same subject, though it is taken in different parts of its extension or its denotation.

The Distribution of the predicate is determined by the *quality* of the proposition, and is not affected by the Distribution of the subject. Beginners find this a difficult point, and part of the difficulty is their natural tendency to regard a proposition as an equation. It cannot be repeated too often that a proposition is *not* an equation. Its predicate[1] does not *equal* its subject, but is affirmed or denied of its subject. The nature of predication decides the distribution of the predicate. *The predicate of affirmative pro-*

---

[1] Sir William Hamilton's doctrine of ' The Quantification of the Predicate ' finds few supporters today. It is discussed by Joseph, *op. cit.*, p. 222 ff.

positions (A and I) is Undistributed ; the predicate of negative propositions (E and O) is Distributed.

These are two-way rules, both of them, and we must be prepared to argue it either way. Given an affirmative proposition, we know that its predicate is undistributed. Given an undistributed predicate, we know that its proposition is affirmative. Given a negative proposition, we know that its predicate is distributed. Given a distributed predicate, we know that its proposition is negative.

The above are the rules for the Distribution of the predicate, which apply to our four ordinary, simple ways of affirming and denying, A, E, I, and O. Learn the rules, apply them, and by degrees you will come to see the reasons for them. Why must the predicate of an affirmative proposition be undistributed ? Why must the predicate of a negative proposition be distributed ? Well, try to break these rules, and you will not find it so easy to do so. Try to make up an affirmation with a distributed predicate ; or try to make up a denial with an undistributed predicate, and you will find either that you cannot do it at all, or that, to do it, you have to depart from our ordinary, simple ways of affirming and denying.

' All philosophers are wise.' The predicate ' wise ' is obviously *un*distributed ; for many other people, besides philosophers, are wise, to say nothing of animals. The affirmation is *about* the subject ; we affirm *wise* about all philosophers. The affirmation is not *about* the predicate *wise* ; we do not affirm anything about *all the wise* ; nor *can* we do so *as long as we are content to talk simply and say one thing at a time*. ' All philosophers are wise '—that simple affirmation *implies* that wise philosophers are *part* of the extension of the term *wise*, but from the nature of affirmation it says nothing and implies nothing as to the *whole* extension of the term *wise*. What holds of this simple affirmation holds of all simple affirmations; therefore the predicate of all A and I propositions must be undistributed.[1]

In a simple denial, on the other hand, like 'No philosophers are fools', the predicate *has* to be taken in its whole extension. Philosophers are excluded from the *whole* class 'fools', or there is no denial. That fact is what makes denials hazardous. The denial is *about* the subject, and is not *about* the predicate, but the denier must know his facts, and must be in a position to exclude his subject from the *whole* extension of the predicate. Therefore the predicate of all E and O propositions must be distributed.

So much for the four standard forms, A, E, I, and O, where the marks of quantity (All, No, and Some) are attached to the subject-term. We will glance now at some less common forms of predication, where the foregoing rules do not apply directly. In propositions of the form 'Only A is B', the predicate is distributed, though the proposition is affirmative, and in those of the form 'A is not the only B' the predicate is undistributed, though the proposition is negative. These are compressed ways of speaking; we are saying two things at once. When we say 'Only philosophers are wise', we are in effect saying, 'Philosophers are wise, and all the wise are philosophers.' 'None but the brave deserve the fair' is equivalent to 'The brave deserve the fair, and all who deserve the fair are brave.'[2] When we say 'The

[1] On affirmative propositions with predicates *accidentally* distributed like 'All equilateral triangles are equiangular', see below (p. 78).
[2] Dryden wrote the line (of Alexander), 'None but the brave deserves the fair', presumably meaning, 'The brave (*sc.* Alexander) deserves the fair, and no one else does.'

English are not the only lovers of sport ', we are implying that the English are lovers of sport, but denying that all the lovers of sport are English.

The beginner should avoid these more complex predications, and should at present confine his attention to the four standard forms, and before proceeding further he should master the rules for the Distribution of Terms, as set forth in the following table :

DISTRIBUTION OF TERMS

	Proposition	Subject	Predicate
A	All S is P	Distributed	Undistributed
E	No S is P	Distributed	Distributed
I	Some S is P	Undistributed	Undistributed
O	Some S is not P	Undistributed	Distributed

The Marks of Quantity

The normal Marks of Quantity are *All*, *No*, and *Some*, as given in the preceding table, and they should be used in elementary work. There are many variants in common speech, requiring attention. In all cases the *sense* of the proposition should be the first consideration.

Often no mark of quantity is expressed. Generalizations of a poetical type, such as ' The grass withereth ; the flower fadeth ' should be read as universals. Whether ' Books are a solace to the weary ' is universal, or meant universally, is arguable. Proverbs are usually universal, and often leave the mark of quantity to the imagination. *He who . . ., They who . . ., Whoever*, usually introduce universals. *Must* and *may*, when quantitative,[1] indicate universals and particulars, respectively. ' Knaves must

[1] On the modal *must* and *may* see below (p. 61).

be fools ' means ' All knaves are fools.' ' The learned may be wise' means 'Some learned are wise.' ' A man may like Logic, and must be the better of it ' is a way of saying, ' Some men like Logic, and all are the better of it.' *Can be* and (in Ireland) *could be* could be particular. ' Parting can be such sweet sorrow ', i.e. ' Some partings are sweet sorrow.' ' Inexpensive salmon could be poached ', i.e. ' Some inexpensive salmon are poached.'

Every is often the equivalent of *All*; where they differ, *Every* is distributive, and *All* collective. ' Every man has his price.' ' All men are fond of money.' *Never* and *Never a* . . . can take the place of *None* or *No*. Particular propositions are often introduced by *A few, most, many*, or by the adverbs, *often, generally, sometimes*.

The formula *All* . . . *not* deserves a special note. Consider the following :

> All things lawful are not expedient.
> All that glitters is not gold.
> All that shivers is not cold.

All three propositions look universal, but are particular. The *All* . . . *not* is an English idiom for *Some* . . . *not*. The same holds of all propositions of that form. They are all O propositions. The point needs careful attention.

What is the justification for this strange idiom ? Why do we say *All* when we mean *Some* ? The first answer is that to say, ' All that glitters is not gold ' is much stronger than to say, ' Some things that glitter are not gold.' And the reason for that additional force is that there is an expectation to be answered, as well as a statement to be made. People *expect* glittering things to be gold, shivering things to be cold, and lawful things to be expedient. We begin with ' All ' in order to answer that presumption.

We deny it by means of the deferred 'not'. We do not say, 'No glittering things are gold'—which would be untrue; but we limit the universality of our own denial, and make it particular by using the formula, *All . . . not*.

Simple, Complex, and Compound Categorical Propositions

He gave me a *categorical* command; that is, he told me to do it without qualification or condition. Similarly, a Categorical Proposition is one stated without qualification or condition. The main variety is the Simple Categorical Proposition, with which we have been dealing till now— S is P, S is not P. These form the backbone of discourse and of the Logic of discourse, and they are usually referred to simply as *propositions*. If the proposition is essentially one predication about one subject, but subject or predicate is complicated by a relative clause or the like, the proposition is sometimes called Complex. Example: 'All who saw the accident or who had other sources of information communicated with Scotland Yard.' The complexity is grammatical; logically it is a straightforward categorical proposition. The term *Complex* is sometimes used to describe Hypothetical and Disjunctive Propositions.

Compound Categorical Propositions are otherwise known as Conjunctive. They consist of two or more categorical propositions, joined by *and* or the equivalent. Examples: 'Rain, hail, snow, and prolonged sunshine put the trout down.' That sentence predicates the same thing of four different subjects; it is four propositions, compounded; for logical treatment they must be set out separately. 'Rain puts the trout down. Hail puts the trout down . . . etc.' 'Neither Arran Chief nor Epicure

C

is suitable for the main-crop.' There we have two categorical denials compounded, ' Arran Chiefs are not suitable for the main-crop ; Epicures are not suitable for the main-crop.'

Sometimes the link is adversative ; it joins by a contrast. Example : ' I am black, but comely.' That sentence would have to be treated as two co-ordinate propositions ' I am black. I am comely '—a poor substitute for the original, but the best that Logic can do. We must not expect Logic to be equal to all the niceties of language. No rational man is always reasoning.

Non-Categorical Propositions

Hypothetical and Disjunctive Propositions make use of categorical predications, but are not themselves categorical ; they connect two or more categorical predications in various ways, but do not themselves predicate anything of a subject categorically. The Hypothetical conjoins the truth of one predication to the truth of another. The Disjunctive disjoins the truth of one or more predications from the truth of one or more predications. Some Hypotheticals can be represented by Categoricals, and Disjunctives can be represented by Hypotheticals ; but in both cases the representation is inadequate. Hypotheticals and Disjunctives are distinct and important ways of making statements. They are in everyday use, and play a considerable part in law and science, and from time immemorial they have been treated as part of Logic.

Hypothetical Propositions

The Hypothetical Proposition states by supposition. If my opponent opens P–K4, says the chess player to himself, I shall play the French Defence, P–K3. If it rains, says the angler, I go a-fishing, and if I go, I shall need rod, reel, book, and creel. If I scorn delights and live laborious days, says the ambitious student, success will be mine. The Hypothetical is in constant use, and, I must add, is being constantly misused by those who have never studied its logical structure and the rules for its use.

The Hypothetical Proposition consists of two predications, of which the one is stated as a supposition or hypothesis or condition, and the other as a consequence; e.g. If A is B, C is D. The supposition (A is B) is called the Antecedent; for it often comes first to the mind and first on the tongue; but the order of expression is neither here nor there. The other predication (C is D) is called the Consequent; it is logically dependent on the Antecedent, and often follows it.

There are two main forms of Hypothetical, (a) Different predicates are affirmed or denied of the one subject. If A is B, it is C. If the wind is from the south, it blows the fly to the fish's mouth, and (b) Different predicates are affirmed or denied of different subjects. If A is B, C is D. If the wind is from the north, the wise angler stays at home.

The word 'if' has various shades of meaning, and the meaning of Hypotheticals varies correspondingly. Sometimes they imply a high degree of doubt, sometimes scarcely any doubt at all. Often 'if' can be replaced by *when* or *where* without substantial change of meaning. Sometimes *if* refers to a particular event or occasion; at other times *if ever* or *if at any time* can be substituted. Sometimes the hypothesis is general, sometimes specific. These considerations affect the question of interchanging Categoricals and Hypotheticals. Each case must be considered on its merits with reference to the content of the proposition. 'Far fields are green' is a pithy equivalent of 'If fields are far, they are green'; but the Hypothetical form expresses the true intent of the proverb.

The Hypothetical Proposition, *as a whole*, is an affirmation; it affirms the dependence of the consequent on the antecedent; but the constituent predications, either or both, may be negative. Examples:

If the barometer does not fall, I shall turn the hay.

If the barometer does not fall, the rain will not come.

Disjunctive Propositions

A Disjunctive Proposition affirms alternatives. It, too, is affirmative as *a whole*, though its constituent clauses may be affirmative or negative. It is a useful form for setting out the constituents of a complex situation without committing yourself to a premature decision. The farmer finds no fruit on his tree. He cannot state the cause for certain; but he can set out the possibilities, and that may help him another year. Either the frost nipped the blossom, or the caterpillar ate the leaf, or the worm devoured the fruit. He states the possibilities disjunctively, i.e. as alternatives. In theory there is no limit to the number of alternatives and the clauses that express them; but for simplicity's sake we will confine ourselves to two.

The terms of the two predications may be disposed in three different ways, and there are three corresponding types of Disjunctive Propositions.

(1) The subject of both is the same and the predicates differ. A is either B or C. He is either a fool or a knave.

(2) The subjects differ, and the predicate is the same. Either A or B is C. Either Oxford or Cambridge won the boat race.

(3) Both subjects differ, and both predicates differ. Either A is B or C is D. Either he stole the money or justice miscarried.[1]

The standing difficulty in disjunctions both in Logic and in life is to know how far the disjoining is meant to be carried. Is it partial or complete? Is it a distinction or a separation? To put the same thing in another way— the word *or*, owing to the native elasticity of living discourse, is ambiguous; it may make the alternatives mutually exclusive, or it may not. The ambiguity is often a convenience, often the reverse, and always a reason for caution where disjunctions are concerned, ' Oatmeal porridge should be eaten with sugar or salt.' Sugar and salt are alternatives. Are they *hard* alternatives? The proposition would be understood in different ways on both sides of the Tweed. Some folk would take it to mean that salt-cellar and sugar-bowl are not *both* required on the breakfast-table; but there are some quite rational people who like both condiments, and they would take a different view. Where the alternatives are not meant to be mutually exclusive, the civil servant shows it by ' and/or ', and the lawyer slips in ' or both '.

The distinction between the two types of disjunction has long been recognized in Logic, and enters into the rules of the Disjunctive Syllogism (see below, p. 149).

[1] N.B. ' Neither . . . nor ' is not the mark of a disjunction, but is the combination of two denials. ' He is neither man nor boy, but a hobbledehoy ' combines two categorical denials with one categorical affirmation.

An attempt has been made to get rid of the ambiguity by altering the traditional names. It has been suggested that the term ' disjunctive ' should be confined to the mutually exclusive type, and that the other type should be called ' Alternative '. The suggestion, however, has not been universally accepted, and it is a ' doubtful improvement ' ; for listing alternatives is the essence of all disjunction. Both types set out alternatives, and to call one type Alternative and not the other is misleading. Moreover both types disjoin, though one type carries the disjoining further than does the other. Logic must adapt itself to discourse, or it becomes illogical. The ambiguity in the word *or* is inherent in the human situation. We shall therefore keep the old name Disjunctive for both types, and where the distinction is necessary, we shall call the one *Exclusive* or *Strong* disjunction, and the other *Non-Exclusive* or *Weak* disjunction.

This is a notable case in which the logic of the *Form* requires a reference to the *Content* (see above, p. 4). There is no way of knowing apart from the Content of the proposition which type of disjunction is intended. ' Either Oxford or Cambridge won the boat race.' The disjunction is *strong*, not because of the *Form* of the proposition, but because of the nature of the race. On the other hand, ' He is a graduate of Oxford or Cambridge ' is by *Form* and *Content* indecisive. Said of a young man, it would probably be a *strong* disjunction ; said of a scholar of established reputation, it might well be *weak*.[1]

An Exclusive Disjunctive Proposition can be resolved

---

[1] In Latin *aut* and *vel* correspond roughly to strong and weak disjunctions, respectively. ' *Aut Caesar aut nullus* ' is a historic example of the former.

into four Hypotheticals. 'A is either B or C (but not both)' can be represented by:

> If A is B, it is not C.
> If A is C, it is not B.
> If A is not B, it is C.
> If A is not C, it is B.

A non-Exclusive Disjunctive Proposition can be resolved into two Hypotheticals. 'A is either B or C, or both' can be represented by:

> If A is not B, it is C.
> If A is not C, it is B.

Modal Propositions

In Modal Propositions the predication is qualified by words such as, *may be, must be, is* (emphatic), *possible, probable, impossible, necessary*. Such words bring the speaker's mind into the proposition, and express his attitude to what he is saying. All propositions are Modal to some slight extent; for we cannot keep ourselves entirely out of what we are saying. The farmer almost succeeded in doing so, who, when congratulated by a townsman on his fine field of turnips, replied, 'Them's mangolds.' He did not mean, they may be, might be, must be, mangolds. He voiced what is called 'the objective fact'. His statement was all about the crop and not about his attitude to it; it was factual, not modal.

Modal propositions are of three main types, Assertoric, Problematic, and Apodeictic. Assertoric Propositions predicate confidently, usually after doubt; e.g. 'Yes, after all; they *are* mangolds.' A Problematic Proposition

states a possibility, viewed as a problem for further study;
e.g. 'Well, they *may* be mangolds.' Apodeictic Propositions imply knowledge with a reason; they aspire after
certainty, attained by reflection and reasoning. Mathematics aims at the ideal of apodeictic certainty. A triangle
not only *may have*, not only *has*, but *must have* its angles
equal to two right angles.

Questions and Exercises on Chapter III

1. Distinguish Propositions from other Sentences.

2. Has a simple Categorical Proposition two parts or three?
Justify your answer. From one point of view, indeed, a
proposition has no parts, but is an indivisible whole?

3. Set out the following propositions in *optimum* logical
form, or as near to it as possible.

(a) Caesar built a bridge over the Rhine.

(b) Oil prospectors take great risks, and may make great
profits.

(c) Golden lads must come to dust.

(d) Prophets teach righteousness.

(e) Alexander Selkirk ruled all he surveyed.

(f) The scholar lives in the past.

(g) Young men see visions, and old men dream dreams.

(h) "The best laid schemes o' mice and men Gang aft
a-gley" (Burns).

(i) Dog won't eat dog.

(j) "A little philosophy inclineth man's mind to atheism
but depth in philosophy bringeth men's minds about
to religion" (Bacon).

4. What is meant by the 'quality' of a proposition? The
quality of most propositions can be altered without seriously
affecting the sense?

5. How is the quantity of a proposition determined? What
is to be done supposing it has no mark of quantity?

6. How is the distribution of the predicate determined?
Can you justify the rules?

7. State the quantity of the following propositions, and the distribution of each term :

(a) All X is Y.

(b) No X is Y.

(c) Some X is Y.

(d) Some X is not Y.

(e) All X is not Y.

(f) All learned men are not wise.

(g) All unlearned men are not foolish.

(h) Rabbits are destructive pests.

(i) Pheasants pick in stubble fields.

(j) Partridge do not take long flights.

8. A, E, I, and O propositions—take one of each ; how many distributed terms have you in all ?

9. How do Hypothetical Propositions differ from Disjunctives ? What types of each may be distinguished ?

10. What are Modal Propositions ?

CHAPTER IV

IMMEDIATE INFERENCE

IN the previous chapter propositions were treated rather like concrete blocks ; we sized them up, sorted them out, and gave technical names to various types. In the present chapter we restore the life and movement they possess ; for in the flow of discourse one proposition passes into another, as wave passes into wave. Robinson Crusoe had no one to talk to aloud ; but when he first saw the tell-tale footprint in the sand, quick as lightning the proposition, ' That's a footprint ' brought into his mind the further proposition, ' A man made it.' That ' bringing in ' of a proposition from one or more propositions is called in Logic Inference.[1]

Inferences are good and bad, valid and invalid. Purists[2] confine the term to good and valid inferences, and there is much in their argument that a bad inference is no inference. But the wider usage suits the logic of life. In life we often meet the hasty inference and the crooked inference ; and it is the task of Logic to halt the hasty and straighten out the crooked. From ' Joab was the son of Zeruiah ' most folk infer that Zeruiah was the father of Joab. That is a hasty inference. Zeruiah was his mother,[3] and her sons evidently drew their sturdy qualities from the distaff side.

---

[1] From the Latin *inferre*, to bring in.
[2] i.e. sticklers for correct usage.
[3] 2 Samuel xvii 25.

The two aspects of Inference

Inference has two aspects; it is both in the mind and in the facts. Inference is an activity of the mind; it is something we do, and know that we do, and do well or ill. We men infer, and often make mistakes in doing so, and need Logic to educate our faculty of inference. But that is not the whole account. We could not draw out the inference, unless it were already there in the facts; we find it, not make it. If we are to infer validly, our inferring must be controlled by the facts, and the facts are propositions to which the mind responds, and which tend to carry the mind forward by their own momentum. The inference *in the facts* is often called implication. Implication is a metaphor from *folding*. The logical inference is viewed as *en*folded in the facts, and *un*folded by the activity of inferring mind.

Immediate and Mediate Inference

Immediate here does not mean *quick*, but *without a middle term*; its opposite is *Mediate*. In Immediate Inference we start from the two terms of a proposition, given true or given false, and without the intervention of any other term we go straight to a second proposition, called the Conclusion, which employs the same two terms. In Mediate Inference, on the other hand, we start from *two* propositions which have one term in common, called the Middle Term, and proceed to a third proposition, called the Conclusion, which employs the other two terms (see below, p. 83).[1]

[1] N.B. Discussion of the Rules of Inference is conducted in the symbolic notation of the four propositional types, A, E, I, O; and at this point the student should look back to the tables on pp. 48

The principal modes of Immediate Inference are, by Subalternation, by Opposition, by Obversion, by Conversion, and by Contraposition. Subalternation can be treated under Opposition, if *Opposition* be understood in a broad sense. The old term *Superalternation*, recently revived, is correct, but is not required here; for where there is a *super* (above) there must be a *sub* (below), and the shorter term has for centuries been recognized as covering both aspects of the relation. N.B. These modes are here treated only in so far as they apply to propositions in one or other of the four standard forms (A, E, I, and O).

Subalternation

Subalternation is the relation existing between two propositions which differ in quantity, but have the same quality, and the same terms as subject and predicate, respectively. The name Subalternation is given also to the inference based on that relation. N.B. By a natural convention the universal is regarded as above (*super*) and the particular as below (*sub*). Examples:

All shepherds seek the good of their flocks.	Some shepherds seek the good of their flocks.
No canals contain running water.	Some canals do not contain running water.
Some patriots are disinterested.	All patriots are disinterested.
Some arts are not crafts.	No arts are crafts.

In symbols the subaltern pairs are: A—I, E—O, I—A, O—E. If we consider any pair of subalterns we see that

and 53, and make sure that he has mastered them, and understands their detail.

both propositions may be true, or both may be false, and that the universal may be false and its particular true. In two cases, and in two cases only, there is material for valid inference, viz. *From the truth of the universal, we may infer the truth of the particular,* and, *From the falsity of the particular, we may infer the falsity of the universal.*

Everyone knows the saying, 'You cannot argue from the particular to the universal', and it is a true saying with regard to arguments *from truth to truth*, but it is not true with regard to arguments *from falsity to falsity*. To argue from ' Some children get mumps ' to ' All children get mumps ' is a downright fallacy. It is the argument from the *truth* of the particular to the *truth* of the universal —a fallacy to which the human mind is as prone as children are to measles and to mumps. On the other hand, to argue from the falsity of ' Some drones gather honey ' to the falsity of ' All drones gather honey ' is perfectly valid. It is a straightforward application of the second rule, stated above, and that rule is plain commonsense. A single drone that does not gather honey is enough to upset the statement that all drones gather honey. Here we are told that it is false that some drones gather honey, which is the same as saying that some drones do not gather it ; and so the statement in question is upset. It is false that all drones gather honey. The same argument applies, whatever the subject and predicate ; if it is false that some students like Logic, it must be false that all students like it. In general, if it is false that some S is P, it must be false that all S is P. In setting out and testing arguments from subalternation we must be careful to state whether the argument is from truth to truth or from falsity to falsity.

Opposition

Opposition is the relation between two propositions which have the same terms as subject and predicate, respectively, but which differ in quality. The name, Opposition, is also given to inference based on that relation. There are three modes of Opposition, Contradiction, Contrariety, and Subcontrariety.

Contradiction

Of two Contradictory Propositions the one affirms what the other denies. They differ both in quality and in quantity. They cannot both be true, nor can they both be false. One of them must be true, and the other must be false. Examples :

CONTRADICTORY PROPOSITIONS

All poets try to please.	Some poets do not try to please.
No poets try to teach.	Some poets try to teach.
" Some books are lies frae end to end."	No books are lies frae end to end.
Some books are not worth binding.	All books are worth binding.

In symbols the contradictory pairs are : A—O, E—I, I—E, O—A.

The rules of Inference are :

(1) From the truth of either contradictory we may infer the falsity of the other.

(2) From the falsity of either contradictory we may infer the truth of the other. Therefore,

If A is true, O is false.
If E is true, I is false.

If I is true, E is false.
If O is true, A is false.
If A is false, O is true.
If E is false, I is true.
If I is false, E is true.
If O is false, A is true.

Contradiction, according to the foregoing rules, is between propositions with a common term as subject; where the subject is a singular term, contradiction is irregular. 'Jack loves Jill' is adequately (for practical purposes) contradicted, however, by 'Jack does not love Jill'.

Contradiction in practice

Logical Contradiction is a precise thing, and not just any form of verbal opposition. If you think that a statement needs contradicting, contradict it; but know the rules and keep them. Contradict the statement rather than the man who made it. 'I shall contradict him flat; there is not a word of truth in what he said.' That is the wrong approach; that is the spirit of all-out opposition—the club, and not the rapier. If it suffices to contradict a statement, it is bad tactics to do more. You will 'go beyond your brief', as the lawyers say, and expose yourself to a damaging counter-attack. Supposing someone says, 'No corporal punishment is justifiable', and you feel the proposition should be contradicted, begin systematically. It is an E proposition; therefore its contradictory is I. 'Some corporal punishment is justifiable.' If you know your justifiable types, then you have sufficiently disproved the statement to which you took exception.

If you go to the opposite extreme and say, 'All corporal punishment is justifiable', you are playing into your opponent's hands, and he will upset your statement by producing some harsh statute of former days, that no one today could defend.

Contrariety

Of two Contrary Propositions the one denies in its whole extent what the other affirms. They cannot both be true, but they may both be false. They must be universal and of different quality, and therefore, in symbols, they are A and E. Examples:

CONTRARY PROPOSITIONS

All Cretans are liars.	No Cretans are liars.
No actions are free.	All actions are free.

The rule of Inference is: From the truth of one Contrary we can infer the falsity of the other.

N.B. Since both Contraries may be false, we cannot argue from falsity to truth, as we can in Contradiction. For instance, if it is false that all punishment is remedial, or that no punishment is remedial, there is no valid inference as to the truth of their Contraries.

The rules of Inference and non-Inference from Contraries can be deduced from those of Subalternation (*s*) and Contradiction (*c*), as follows:

If A is true, I is true (by *s*); therefore E is false (by *c*).
If A is true, O is false (by *c*); therefore E is false (by *s*).

If E is true, O is true (by *s*); therefore A is false (by *c*).
If E is true, I is false (by *c*); therefore A is false (by *s*).

If A is false, O is true (by *c*); thence there is no inference as to E.

If E is false, I is true (by *c*); thence there is no inference as to A.

Subcontrariety

Of two Subcontrary Propositions the one affirms particularly what the other denies particularly. They may both be true; they cannot both be false. Being both particular and differing in quality, they are, in symbols, I and O. Examples:

SUBCONTRARY PROPOSITIONS

Some rivers are alkaline.	Some rivers are not alkaline.
Some slow driving is not good driving.	Some slow driving is good driving.

The rule of Inference is: From the falsity of either Subcontrary we may infer the truth of the other.

N.B. Since both Subcontraries may be true, we cannot argue from truth to falsity, as in Contrariety. The rules of Inference and non-Inference can be deduced from those of subalternation and contradiction, as follows:

If I is false, E is true (by *c*); therefore O is true (by *s*).

If O is false, A is true (by *c*); therefore I is true (by *s*).

If I is true, E is false (by *c*); thence there is no inference as to O.

If O is true, A is false (by *c*); thence there is no inference as to I.

These rules can be deduced also from those of Contradiction and Contrariety, as follows : If possible, let I and O both be false ; then their contradictories E and A must both be true ; but E and A are contraries, which cannot both be true. Therefore I and O cannot both be false ; i.e. if I is false, O is true, and if O is false, I is true.

On the other hand, if I and O are both true, their contradictories E and A are both false, which is consistent with the rules of contrariety.

Aristotle[1] suggested that there is no real opposition between subcontraries, because, for example, those rivers that are acid are not those that are alkaline ; but rivers are rivers, acid or alkaline. Terms have connotation as well as denotation and extension (see above, p. 23). The two subcontraries are distinguished and contrasted, if not actually opposed, and they have, in fact, one common subject, taken in different parts of its extension or of its denotation.

The following ancient diagram, known as ' Aristotle's Square ' or (less correctly) as ' The Square of Opposition,'

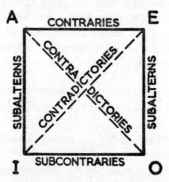

[1] *Analytica Priora*, II, 15, 63b 27.

shows graphically the relations between propositions under Subalternation and Opposition.

The other Modes of Immediate Inference

Before we consider in detail Obversion, Conversion, and Contraposition, there are one or two general points to be noted. These three Modes rank with the two already explained as processes essential to the logic of the syllogism. This trio, however, is not quite on all fours with the other two. Obversion, Conversion, and Contraposition rest on relations, as do Subalternation and Opposition, but in themselves they are active mental processes consciously aimed at inference. They make changes in the given; some of the processes alter quality, turning affirmations into denials, and denials into affirmations; some of the processes displace both terms, turning subject into predicate and predicate into subject. How can these changes be justified, and how can inferences that rest on them be valid? The answer brings us back to a truth which is always in danger of being overlooked, namely the unity of the whole proposition. The proposition is an organic unity. The logician analyses, as the anatomist dissects. He breaks up the proposition into subject and predicate, and treats them as separate parts; but in actual discourse the parts are not separate, and the proposition is an organic whole. 'Man is mortal' is not the bare association of two separate terms, *man* and *mortal*; it is the assertion of one truth—the mortality of mankind. Within the limits of that truth we may change the outward form of that assertion, and all such changes are justified. Inferences that rest upon the assertion in its changed form rest upon 'the given', and are valid.

Obversion

In Obversion, otherwise known as Permutation, the quality of the proposition is changed, and for the predicate its contradictory term (see above, p. 22) is substituted; the meaning of the proposition remains substantially unaltered. The given proposition is called the Obvertend; the derived proposition is called the Obverse. Obvertend and Obverse should be equipollent. They have the same subject, and much the same thing is predicated of it in both propositions; but the one affirms the predicate, while the other denies its contradictory.

To obvert a proposition proceed as follows: (1) Leave the subject and its quantity as they are, (2) Substitute for the predicate its contradictory, (3) Change the quality thus, (a) in A and I propositions attach a *not* to the copula, (b) in E and O propositions omit the *not* (or its equivalent) from the copula. The given proposition must be in full logical form with the copula expressed (see above, p. 39); established contradictories, like *untrue*, *irrational*, etc., should be used in preference to compounds with *not* or *non*. When introducing a *not* into an A proposition, beware of the trap, 'All . . . not' (see above, p. 54). When practised in the elementary method, the student should obvert with a freer hand, taking care to secure substantial equivalence. Examples:

Obvertend	*Obverse*
All S is P.	No S is not-P.
No S is P.	All S is not-P.
Some S is P.	Some S is not not-P.
Some S is not P.	Some S is not-P.
All men are reasonable.	No men are unreasonable.
No tigers are merciful.	All tigers are merciless.

Obvertend	*Obverse*
Some rebukes are deserved.	Some rebukes are not un-deserved.
Some conifers are not decidu-ous.	Some conifers are not-decidu-ous, *or*
	Some conifers keep their leaves in winter.
All textbooks on logic are not suitable for beginners.	Some textbooks on logic are unsuitable for beginners.
No women live on Mt. Athos.	[1] The entire population of Mt. Athos is male.
No men are admitted.	All men are excluded.
Some tongues wag too freely.	Some people do not curb their tongues.
Some ills are not wholly evil.	[1] It's an ill wind that blows no one any good.

Absolute equivalence of Obvertend and Obverse is only to be had with abstract symbols, and there the equivalence is purely formal. In the other examples, given above, a slight difference in meaning or tone will be detected; for an affirmation, however offset in the predicate, can hardly ever have quite the same force as a denial (see on Equipollence above, p. 45).

Conversion

Conversion is the interchange of the subject and the predicate, so that the original subject becomes the predicate, and the original predicate becomes the subject. The original proposition is called the Convertend; the derived proposition is called the Converse. The convertend and

---

[1] These two examples of *free* obversion may be questioned, but can be justified on the ground that the obverse puts positively in substance what the obvertend puts negatively. The former example is almost an 'obverted converse' (see below, p. 78).

the converse have the same quality ; they may, or may not, differ in quantity.

No term which is undistributed in the convertend may be distributed in the converse. This is the rule of rules. The student should memorize it, should practise applying it, and should try to understand the reason for it. Let us study a breach of this rule which is all too common. In some circles, where Logic is undervalued, it is a short step in argument from, say, ' All learned men are wise ' to ' All wise men are learned.' It is a short step, but an utterly false step ; and what is wrong is that the inference goes beyond the *given*. In the *given* the term *wise* is undistributed (being the predicate of an affirmation) ; in the inference it is distributed ; from a proposition, given true, connecting the learned with *some* wise men, we have ' deduced ' a proposition connecting the learned with *all* wise men ; we have no ground for the ' deduction ', and the supposed inference proves to be a fallacy. In inference we must not take from the *given* more than is there to take. This is the fundamental principle of all inference, mediate or immediate.

It is a one-way rule, be it noted ; and beginners are apt to take it both ways. The rule does *not* state that terms must have the same quantity in convertend and converse ; and there is nothing against a term, distributed in the convertend, being undistributed in the converse, as with *learned* in the instance given above. In a word, what we take out of the *given* may be *less* than is given ; but must not be *more*.

There are two modes of Conversion, as defined above, *Simple* and *Per Accidens*. When the quantity of the converse is the same as that of the convertend, Conversion is Simple. Only E and I propositions convert simply.

When the convertend is universal, and the converse particular, Conversion is *Per Accidens*. Only A propositions convert *Per Accidens*. The Latin name is opposed to *per se*, which means *essential*. When the converse is particular, it is regarded as dealing with unessential, accidental attributes. O propositions cannot be converted, and this breach of symmetry has often led logicians to widen the definition of Conversion, so as to make it include Contraposition. Examples:

SIMPLE CONVERSION

Convertend	*Converse*
No S is P (E).	No P is S (E).
No proteins are free from nitrogen.	No things free from nitrogen are proteins.
No fish stir in our heaving nets.	No things that stir in our heaving nets are fish.
Some S is P (I).	Some P is S (I).
Some turf is combustible.	Some combustible material is turf.
Some 'drag' hunts are monotonous.	Some monotonous occupations are 'drag' hunts.
New brooms may sweep clean.	Some efficient workers are new brooms.

CONVERSION *Per Accidens*

Convertend	*Converse*
All S is P (A).	Some P is S (I).
All sugars are soluble in water.	Some things soluble in water are sugars.
All followers of Izaak Walton love virtue and angling.	Some who love virtue and angling are followers of Izaak Walton.

If we try to convert A propositions *simply*, we break the fundamental rule, and make the undistributed predicate of the convertend into the distributed subject of the converse. This is a common mistake in hasty argument, especially when the marks of quantity are not expressed.

In mathematics and occasionally elsewhere we may come on A propositions which *appear* to convert simply, but do not really do so; e.g.

> All equilateral triangles are equiangular.
> All equiangular triangles are equilateral.

The two propositions are established independently, or they both flow from the one definition. The one is not an inference from the other. The true converse of 'All equilateral triangles are equiangular' is 'Some equiangular figures are equilateral triangles.'

Conversion of Singular Propositions

Singular propositions cannot be converted where only the subject is singular; e.g. Great is Diana of the Ephesians. We can alter the order of the words, but we cannot transpose subject and predicate. Where both terms are singular, conversion is possible in theory; e.g. 'Tully is Cicero' becomes 'Cicero is Tully'; but this change is little more than verbal.

Obversion of the Converse

The obverted converse has for its subject the original predicate, and for its predicate the contradictory of the original subject. The inference to the obverted converse is valid. N.B. O propositions have no converse. Examples:

Convertend	Converse	Obverted Converse
All S is P	Some P is S	Some P is not not-S
No S is P	No P is S	All P is not-S
Some S is P	Some P is S	Some P is not not-S

Contraposition

Contraposition consists in first obverting, and then converting the obverse. The chief use of the process is to alter the quality of a negative convertend; it transfers the negation to the predicate, and thus enables the converse to admit an undistributed predicate. In this way it does for O propositions what conversion proper cannot do.

A is contraposed simply; for its obverse is E.
E is contraposed *per accidens*; for its obverse is A.
I cannot be contraposed; for its obverse is O.
O can be contraposed simply; for its obverse is I.

Examples:

Original	Contrapositive
All S is P.	No not-P is S.
No S is P.	Some not-P is S.
Some S is not P.	Some not-P is S.
All safe weed-killers are selective.	No non-selective preparations are safe weed-killers.
All mistakes are excusable.	Nothing inexcusable is a mistake.
No Arabs are inhospitable.	Some hospitable people are Arabs.
No incunabula were published later than A.D. 1500.	Some books, not published later than A.D. 1500, are incunabula.
No legends are historical.	Some unhistorical tales are legends.
Some spaniels do not retrieve.	Some dogs that do not retrieve are spaniels.
Some remedies are not pleasant.	Some unpleasant things are remedies.

In all these cases the original subject is the predicate

of the contrapositive, and the contradictory of the original predicate is its subject. No further process is required in syllogistic logic; but contraposition can be carried a stage further, by obverting the contrapositives, yielding as the inferred predicate the contradictory of the original subject.

Other forms of Non-syllogistic Inference

(1) *Inversion*

Inversion is a complex process by which from one proposition (the Invertend) another (the Inverse) is inferred, having as its subject the contradictory of the original subject. Inversion proceeds by twice alternately obverting and converting the invertend, beginning with obversion in the case of A, and with conversion in the case of E. In the cases of I and O inverses are not obtainable.[1]

(2) *Inference by Added or Subtracted Determinants and Complex Conception*

These designations are given to inferences, based on informal arguments, which we intuitively see to be valid. They are hard to classify; but some of them, such as ' A negro is a man; therefore a sick negro is a sick man ' can be explained as extensions of the principle of Subalternation (Substitution). The argument, ' A red ant is a red insect; therefore an ant is an insect ' is of this type. Arguments like, Foxes rob hen-roosts; therefore those who hunt foxes hunt the robbers of hen-roosts, or, Jonah was one of the minor prophets; therefore the whale that

[1] Inversion is a logical exercise of little practical value, but of considerable theoretical importance; for it appears to issue in the fallacy known as Illicit Process. It brings up the question of the existential import of propositions.

swallowed him swallowed one of the minor prophets, are judged valid on practical grounds.

Questions and Exercises on Chapter IV

1. Distinguish Immediate inference from Mediate.

2. What inferences by Subalternation are legitimate?

3. Explain the difference between Contradictory and Contrary Opposition. Which is the safer weapon in controversy?

4. Contradict:
Shorn lambs feel the cold.
Winds are not tempered to shorn lambs.
No lambs are shorn.
All books are valuable.
All books are not valuable.
Military service is a necessary evil in time of peace.
To vote is the first duty of a citizen.
No incunabula are written by hand.
Some hae meat that canna eat. (Is there any doubt as to which term is subject, and which predicate?)
Some psychological facts are significant, some not.
The Tories are always right.

5. Give the Contrary of:
Every cloud has a silver lining.
No policemen carry firearms.
All politicians compromise.
No snow falls on high seas.
The King can do no wrong.

6. Deduce the rules of Inference and non-Inference from Contraries from those of Subalternation and Contradiction.

7. Obvert:
All A is B.
No A is B.
Some A is B.
Some A is not B.
All bicycles require oiling.
All sailors are handy men.

Top hats never go out of fashion.
Some partings are sweet sorrows.
Some sunny days are not good washing days.

8. Truth always triumphs. This opinion has triumphed. Therefore it is true. Is the inference valid? If not, why not?

9. Write a note on Inversion.

10. Convert:
Brutus killed Caesar.
All tax-payers have the vote.
No aliens have the vote.
Cigarettes for the troops are not dutiable.

11. Contrapose:

Some birds cannot fly.
All that glitters is not gold.
Not all lawyers are barris-ters.
Some wines are not dutiable.

Some marmalade is not made with oranges.
All snakes are not poisonous.
Some logicians do not class Contraposition under Conversion.

CHAPTER V

THE SYLLOGISM

THE Syllogism is composed of propositions, which in turn are composed of terms, and its structure should be considered and described as made up both of propositions and of terms.

A Syllogism is a triad of connected propositions, so related that one of them, called the Conclusion, necessarily follows from the other two, which are called the Premisses. That is the simpler and easier description.

The other description is more penetrating and more instructive. *A Syllogism is an argument to prove[1] that two terms which are each related, as subject or as predicate, to the same third term, are necessarily related, as subject or as predicate, to one another.*

The two descriptions are complementary. The syllogism must have three subject-predicate propositions, two to join terms 1 and 2 to the same third term, and one to join them to one another. Thus, suppose we wish to construct an argument to prove that the two terms *unselfish* and *happy*, which are each related, as subject or as predicate, to the same third term *good*, are necessarily related, as subject or as predicate, to one another, three propositions suggest themselves at once, and together constitute (in outline) a syllogism, the first two propositions, which relate the two terms to the same third term, being the premisses, and the third proposition

---

[1] i.e. proving, or at least purporting to prove, in a particular case. On ' invalid inferences ' which include ' invalid syllogisms ', see above, p. 64.

which relates the two terms to one another being the
conclusion :

> The good are happy.
> The unselfish are good.
> Therefore[1] the unselfish are happy.

Aristotle defined syllogism as " discourse in which,
certain things being stated, something other than what
is stated follows of necessity from their being so ".[2]
The mesh of the definition is too wide, and would let in
non-syllogistic inferences ; in other respects it well
describes the three essentials of a syllogism, (1) The *data*,
the ' things stated ', i.e. the premisses, (2) The result or
conclusion, the ' something other ', and (3) The necessity
of the consequence.

Syllogistic Inference is known as Mediate, because it
hinges on the ' third term ', known as the Middle Term,
the *Medius Terminus*. The word *syllogism* comes from the
Greek συλλογισμός, which originally meant a reckoning up
and which later came to mean reasoning in general. To
syllogize is thus by derivation and usage ' to put two and
two together ' in regulated discourse, and to gather from
them (in Aristotle's phrase) ' something other '. There
are other ways of reasoning ;[3] but men do syllogize and
reason in syllogisms ; and the logic of the syllogism is
to the average man of education a gymnasium in which to

---

[1] From this on, the word *Therefore* when it marks the formal conclusion of a syllogism, will be represented by the sign of the three
dots ∴ .

[2] *Analytica Priora*, I, 1, 24b.

[3] e.g. judgments of comparative size or quantity, such as, ' A is
greater than B, B is greater than C, ∴ A is greater than C ' ; or
judgments of equality, such as, ' A is equal to B, B is equal to C,
∴ A is equal to C ' ; or, again arguments *a fortiori* ; such as, " If
God so clothe the grass of the field . . . shall He not much more
clothe you . . ."—Matthew vi 30.

study and practise the finer points of reasoning. The structure of the syllogism is neat, and its Figures and Moods, with their Rules, form a notable chain or network of close argument comparable to Euclidean geometry in clarity and cogency. The syllogism is a test for consistency; it can furnish proof for propositions, accepted or disputed, and it can be an instrument for ascertaining new truth. Syllogizing helps a man to seek and find truth; for conscious syllogizing, conducted in a liberal spirit, is a general tonic for the mind. Disguised syllogisms occur in ordinary discourse. A knowledge of syllogistic technique curbs hasty inference, disciplines slovenly thought, promotes precise statement, clears up ambiguities, and corrects fallacies. Syllogizing encourages a man to seek premisses, to examine them, and to value good premisses; and it is first-class training in drawing conclusions and testing them.

Truth and Validity

This distinction, made at the outset (p. 2), is of special importance here; for in the study of the syllogism, as such, Logic concentrates on the form of the reasoning, for the most part, and is not directly concerned with the truth of its contents. If the syllogism complies with the formal rules, it is valid; if not, not. If the conclusion follows from the premisses, the conclusion is valid, and the syllogism, as such, is valid, even though premiss and conclusion may not be true to fact. Example:

> All fish are cold-blooded.
> Whales are fish.
> ∴ Whales are cold-blooded.

The first premiss is true; the second is false; the conclusion is false; but the conclusion is correctly drawn from the premisses, and is therefore valid in its syllogism, even though it is not true to fact.

The reverse can happen, too. A proposition, true to fact, may appear as the conclusion of an invalid syllogism. Example:

> The industrious are prudent.
> Ants are prudent.
> ∴ Ants are industrious.

These examples are warnings against the habit of judging the validity or invalidity of a syllogism by the truth or falsity of the conclusion. As students of Logic our first duty is to look at the *working* of the syllogism, and to judge its validity, or otherwise, by the rules. No good comes of confusing the two sets of terms, as is sometimes done. Truth is truth, and validity is validity, and neither term can do duty for the other. The lazy habit of styling a *valid* conclusion true, or a true conclusion *valid*, weakens both our sense of truth and our feeling for logic.

The three connected propositions to make a syllogism must comply with the following structural conditions: (*a*) Their terms, numerically six, must be in fact three terms, each occurring twice, (*b*) The subject of the conclusion must occur in one of the premisses, (*c*) The predicate of the conclusion must occur in the other premiss, (*d*) The third term, known as the Middle term, must occur in both premisses, but not in the conclusion. With the above disposition of terms, the syllogism is a connected whole; for the Middle term joins the two premisses together, and the two other terms join the premisses to the conclusion.

The following technical terms should be noted. The subject of the conclusion is called the Minor term, and the premiss that contains it is the Minor Premiss. The predicate of the conclusion is called the Major term, and the premiss that contains it is the Major Premiss. The Major and Minor terms, when spoken of together, are called the Extremes. The Conclusion before it is proved is known as the Question.

The allocation of the names, Major and Minor, was made by Aristotle, and is universally accepted. In some cases it is arbitrary, in others not. In a conclusion, like 'Some students are athletes', it is arbitrary. The term *students* is not minor in relation to *athletes*, nor is the term *athletes* major in relation to *students*. Aristotle when he assigned the names had principally in mind 'scientific' conclusions, like 'All cows are ruminants', where the predicate describes an important feature of the subject, and extends beyond it to other subjects.

N.B. The order of the three propositions has nothing to say to the validity of the syllogism. The accepted order is Major Premiss, Minor Premiss, Conclusion. The student should observe that order, at any rate at first.

The Middle Term is the hinge of the syllogism; without it the premisses would fall apart, and no mediate inference would be possible. The name goes back to Aristotle who named it so, because he wrote it in the middle. He normally wrote his syllogisms in the form, 'P is predicated of M. M is predicated of S. P is predicated of S.' Probably, too, he thought of it as coming midway in meaning, as well as in position.

D

The General Rules[1]

The General Rules of syllogism, as here listed, are seven in number. The number can be increased by regarding structural features as Rules. The *General Rules*, as distinct from the *Special Rules*, are those that apply to all syllogisms, irrespective of Figure. They are :

(1) *The middle term must be distributed at least once.*

If the middle term is not distributed at least once, it cannot serve the purpose of a middle term; it cannot bring the extremes together ; for it might be taken in one part of its extension in one premiss, and in a different part of its extension in the other premiss ; and then the premisses would fall asunder. Example :

> Fat men can swim.
> Jones can swim.
> ∴ Jones is a fat man.

There are fat swimmers and lean swimmers, and there is nothing in the premisses to show to which part of the extension of *swimmers* Jones belongs. The corresponding fallacy (see below, p. 160) is called Undistributed Middle.

(2) *No term, undistributed in its premiss, may be distributed in the conclusion.*

A statement, given true of a term in respect of part only of its extension or denotation, need not be true of the rest. The same point is explained above (p. 76) with regard to Immediate Inference.

A breach of this rule is known as Illicit Process, which may be of the Major term, or of the Minor term. N.B.

---

[1] The two rules for the distribution of the predicate (above, p. 50) play a large part in the proofs of these Rules, and the student should refer to them.

This rule does not require a term to have the *same* quantity in premiss and conclusion. There is nothing against a term, distributed in its premiss, being undistributed in the conclusion, except that in such cases one is generally entitled to conclude about *all*; and if one is entitled to conclude about *all*, it is usually (but not always) pointless to conclude about *some*.

Corollary. From Rules 1 and 2, taken together, it follows that *There must be at least one more distributed term in the premisses than in the conclusion*. For a term distributed in the conclusion must have been distributed in its premiss, and in addition the premisses contain the middle term, at least once distributed.

The next three rules concern Quality.

(3) *From two negative premisses nothing follows*. If one man says, ' A is not B ', and another adds, ' B is not C ', no advance is registered. Nothing has been affirmed. A and C have been excluded from B; but that does not include A in C, or exclude A from C. The data do not relate A and C positively or negatively. The universality of this rule has been challenged from time to time, and there are notable discussions of it in the *Port Royal Logic* and in Keynes' *Logic*.[1] The gist of these discussions is that where cases occur of two negative premisses, apparently yielding a valid conclusion, either one of the premisses is a disguised affirmation, or there are four terms, or in some other way the inference is non-syllogistic. There are no good grounds for doubting the universality of Rule 3.

(4) *From two affirmative premisses a negative conclusion cannot follow*. In other words, if the conclusion is negative, one of the premisses must be negative. For when

[1] J. N. Keynes, *Formal Logic*, 4th ed., p. 295.

both premises are affirmative, the extremes include or are included in the middle term; but that can give no ground for asserting that the one extreme *excludes* the other.

(5) *If either premiss is negative, the conclusion is negative.* In this case the one premiss is affirmative, and the other negative; that is to say, the one extreme includes, or is included in, the middle term, and the other extreme excludes, or is excluded from the middle term. If anything follows, it must be the exclusion of the one extreme from the other, not the inclusion of the one extreme in the other; it must be the denial of relation between them, not the affirmation of relation between them.

The next (and last) two rules concern Quantity.

(6) *From two particular premisses nothing follows.* Suppose it possible that there could be two particular premisses. These must be II, IO, OI, or OO. II contains no distributed term and is excluded by Rule 1. IO and OI contain only one distributed term apiece, and are excluded because by Rule 5 the conclusions of both must be negative, and their predicates distributed, and therefore by the Corollary of Rules 1 and 2 *two* distributed terms apiece in the premisses would be required. OO is excluded by Rule 3.

(7) *If either premiss is particular, the conclusion is particular. First case.* Both premisses are affirmative. These must be A and I, which between them have only *one* distributed term, and *two* would be required by the above Corollary, if the conclusion were universal. The conclusion therefore is particular. *Second case.* One of the premisses is negative. The pairs must be either AO or EI. Each of these pairs contains only two distributed terms, and since the conclusions are negative, *three* would be

required by the Corollary, if the conclusions were universal. Therefore the conclusions are particular.

N.B. The General Rules should be mastered before the student goes on to the Figures and their Special Rules.

The Figures of Syllogism

All syllogisms have a common structure, as explained above; but within that structure there are four varieties, called Figures, determined by the varying position of the middle term. It can be subject of both premisses, predicate of both premisses, subject of the major and predicate of the minor, or predicate of the major and subject of the minor. Thus arithmetically four Figures are possible, and four Figures are taught. The Fourth Figure, however, does not rank with the other three, and Aristotle did not recognize it, though he knew of it. The Schemata of the Four Figures are as follows:

First Figure	Second Figure	Third Figure	Fourth Figure
M P	P M	M P	P M
S M	S M	M S	M S
———	———	———	———
S P	S P	S P	S P

It assists the visual memory to take the arrangement of terms in the First Figure as typical, as in a sense (see below, p. 109) it is, and to note that in the Second Figure, the major premiss, in the Third Figure the minor premiss, and in the Fourth Figure both premisses, vary from the type. The Fourth Figure exactly reverses the typical order.

When the General Rules of syllogism are applied to the peculiarities of each Figure, a new set of rules emerges which are called the *Special Rules*. The seven General

Rules apply to all syllogisms, just as school rules apply to every member of the school. In addition each of the Four Figures has its own Special Rules which apply to every syllogism in that figure, just as, in addition to school rules, classes in the school have their own class rules, which apply to every member of the class.

The best way to master the Special Rules is to work out on paper the proof of each rule with the Schema of each Figure before one's eyes. After a little practice the sight of the Schema suggests the appropriate rules. For instance, as soon as we see the two predicate 'M's in the Second Figure, we see that one of the premisses must be negative in order to give a distributed middle term.

Special Rules of the First Figure

(1) The minor premiss must be affirmative. M P
(2) The major premiss must be universal. S M
———
S P

Proofs. Suppose the minor to be negative; then the major would be affirmative (by G.R.3) and its predicate undistributed, *and* the conclusion would be negative (by G.R.5) and its predicate distributed; but in the first figure the predicate of the conclusion is the predicate of the major. The supposition of a negative minor thus results in a fallacy, the Illicit Process of the Major; it requires the major term to be undistributed in the premiss and distributed in the conclusion; which is absurd. Therefore the minor must be affirmative.

The second rule is proved from the first. Since the minor is affirmative, its predicate, the middle term, is undistributed; the middle term is therefore distributed in the major (by G.R.1). It is subject of the major, which is therefore universal.

N.B. In the first figure both extremes occupy the same position, respectively, in the premiss and in the conclusion. This accounts for the special clearness of most first figure syllogisms. Example:

> All men are mortal.
> Heroes are men.
> ∴ Heroes are mortal.

Special Rules of the Second Figure

(1) One of the premisses must be negative. P M
(2) The major premiss must be universal. S M
                                          ———
                                           S P

Proofs. The middle term is predicate of both premisses, and if both were affirmative, the middle term would be undistributed in both—a breach of G.R.1. The second rule is proved from the first. Since one of the premisses is negative, the conclusion must be negative (by G.R.5), and its predicate distributed. The predicate of the conclusion is subject of the major, which is therefore universal.

N.B. In the second figure the minor term occupies the same position in premiss and conclusion, and the major term occupies a different position in premiss and conclusion. Example:

> No fish have lungs.
> Whales have lungs.
> ∴ Whales are not fish.

Special Rules of the Third Figure

(1) The minor premiss must be affirmative. M P

(2) The conclusion must be particular. M S

————

S P

Proofs. For proof of the first rule see proof of the same rule in the first figure (p. 92). The second rule follows from the first. Since the minor is affirmative, its predicate is undistributed; its predicate is subject of the conclusion, which is therefore particular.

N.B. In the third figure the major term occupies the same position in premiss and conclusion; the minor term occupies a different position in premiss and conclusion. Example :

All educated men tolerate opposition.

Some educated men are impulsive.

∴ Some impulsive men tolerate opposition.

Special Rules of the Fourth Figure

They are three in number, and are all con- P M
ditional, arguing from quality to quantity. M S

————

S P

(1) If the major premiss is affirmative, the minor premiss is universal.

(2) If the minor premiss is affirmative, the conclusion is particular.

(3) If a premiss is negative, the major premiss is universal.

Proofs. (1) If the major is affirmative, its predicate, the middle term, is undistributed. The middle term in the minor must therefore be distributed (by G.R.1). It is subject of the minor, which must therefore be universal.

(2) If the minor is affirmative, its predicate, the minor term, is undistributed, and is therefore undistributed in the conclusion (by G.R.2), which is therefore particular.

(3) If one premiss is negative, the conclusion is negative (by G.R.5), and its predicate distributed. The major term must therefore be distributed in its premiss (by G.R.2), where it is subject. The major premiss must therefore be universal.

N.B. In the fourth figure both extremes occupy different positions, respectively, in premiss and conclusion. Aristotle regarded the fourth as an inverted first figure. Its acceptance as a distinct figure is erroneously attributed to Galen, the celebrated Greek physician, and it is named after him the Galenian Figure. Example:

A strictly forbidden thing is smoking.
All smoking is pleasant.
∴ Some pleasant things are strictly forbidden.

The Moods of Syllogism[1]

Syllogisms are classified still further by their Moods. Mood, from the Latin *modus*, is the determination of the syllogism according to the quality and the quantity of its constituent propositions. Each of the three propositions is designated by its appropriate vowel, A, E, I, or O, and the three vowels, written consecutively in the conventional syllogistic order—major premiss, minor premiss, conclusion—designate the Mood of the syllogism. Thus an AAA syllogism is one with three universal affirmative

[1] For the so-called *indirect* Moods see Joseph, *op. cit.*, pp. 268–9.

propositions. An EAE syllogism is one with a universal negative major, a universal affirmative minor, and a universal negative conclusion.

Mood Names have developed naturally from Mood vowels. An AAA syllogism can occur only in the first figure; an EAE syllogism can occur in the first or second figures. An EIO syllogism can occur in any of the four figures. In order to distinguish mood from mood within the figure, and at the same time to designate both the figure and the mood, the mood vowels have from time immemorial been incorporated into Mood Names, different names with the same vowels being used to indicate the different figures. Thus the mood vowels EAE are incorporated into the mood name Celarent in the first figure, and into Cesare in the second figure; and Celarent and Cesare are the mood names for EAE syllogisms in the first and second figures, respectively. Similarly, Ferio, Festino, Ferison, and Fresison are the mood names for EIO syllogisms of the first, second, third, and fourth figures, respectively.

Mood names, fashioned on the same principle, have long[1] been bestowed on every valid mood in all four figures. Most of them are cleverly devised, and have a Latin air about them, though they are Latin words only *per accidens*. They have been collected and versified in the mnemonic lines which follow. The mood names are printed in italics; the other words are merely a Latin framework. The meaning is roughly, ' The moods Barbara, etc. are of the first figure. Cesare, etc. are of the second figure. The third figure has Darapti, etc. The fourth adds Bramantip, etc.'

[1] Apparently since the thirteenth century; see historical note in Joseph, *op. cit.*, p. 267.

Bărbără, Cēlārēnt, Dărĭĭ, Fĕrĭōquĕ prĭōris.
Cēsărĕ, Cāmēstrēs, Fēstīnŏ, Bărōcŏ, sĕcūndae.
Tērtĭă *Dārāptĭ, Dĭsămĭs, Dătīsĭ, Fĕlāpton*
Bōcārdŏ, Fērĭsŏn hăbēt ; quārta īnsŭpĕr āddit
Brāmāntīp, Cămĕnēs, Dĭmārĭs, Fēsāpŏ, Frēsīson.[1]

Deduction of the Moods

Owing to the differing positions of the terms, moods possible in one figure are not possible in another figure. To find out which moods are valid in each figure we proceed to deduce them from the General Rules and the Special Rules, using the Method of Elimination.

Sixteen pairs of premisses are possible mathematically ; for each of the four letters (A, E, I, and O), representing the major, could combine with each of the same four, representing the minor. Of these sixteen, seven pairs, viz. EE, EO, II, IO, OE, OI, OO, are excluded by the rules against two negatives and two particulars. In addition IE is excluded by G.R.2 ; for the major term is distributed in the negative conclusion, but would have to be undistributed in the I premiss.

The remaining eight possible pairs, viz. AA, AE, AI, AO, EA, EI, IA, OA, must now be tried in each figure.

First Figure. AE and AO are excluded by the first Special Rule, and IA and OA by the second. That leaves AA, AI, EA, and EI as possible pairs of premisses in the first figure. Now consider the conclusions possible with

[1] The lines should be memorized ; for they are packed with meaning, as will appear later. To assist memory let me add that the lines are metrical. The metre is the hexameter, familiar to readers of Virgil. " How art thou fallen from heaven, O Lucifer, son of the morning ! " (Isaiah xiv 12) is a Biblical hexameter which may help those who do not read Latin to give the right stresses. The long (—) vowels and the short (‿) are marked above.

each pair. AA and AI require affirmative conclusions, EA and EI require negative conclusions, and AI and EI require particular conclusions. The possible moods thus are : AAA, (AAI), AII, EAE(EAO), and EIO. Where it is legitimate to draw the conclusions A and E, it is also legitimate to draw the conclusions I and O, respectively ; and therefore the moods AAA and EAE in the ordinary way render the moods AAI and EAO unnecessary ; the latter pair are known as ' Weakened moods ' or ' Subaltern moods ', and are not included in the list. The valid moods left then are AAA, EAE, AII, and EIO, which have received the names Barbara, Celarent, Darii, and Ferio, respectively.

Second Figure. AA, AI, and IA are excluded by the first Special Rule, and IA and OA by the second. That leaves AE, AO, EA, and EI as possible pairs of premisses ; these could yield six moods ; but, as before, disregarding the ' weakened ' moods, we are left with four valid moods, EAE, AEE, EIO, and AOO, which have received the names Cesare, Camestres, Festino, and Baroco, respectively.

Third Figure. AE and AO are excluded by the first Special Rule. That leaves AA, AI, EA, EI, IA, and OA as possible pairs of premisses ; these yield six valid moods, viz. AAI, AII, EAO, EIO, IAI, and OAO, which have received the names Darapti, Datisi, Felapton, Ferison, Disamis, and Bocardo, respectively.

Fourth Figure. AI and AO are excluded by the first Special Rule, and OA by the third. That leaves AA, AE, EA, EI, IA as possible pairs of premisses ; these could yield six valid moods, but disregarding the ' weakened mood ' AEO, we are left with five, viz. AAI, AEE, EAO, EIO, and IAI, which have received the names Bramantip, Camenes, Fesapo, Fresison, and Dimaris, respectively.

Questions and Exercises on Chapter V

1. Explain the structure of the syllogism. Why are the major and minor terms so called? How did the middle term get its name? What is its function?

2. List the General Rules of Syllogism. Why are they called ' General '?

3. The premisses must contain at least one more distributed term than the conclusion. Why?

4. What determines the Figure of Syllogism? Give the schemata of the Four Figures, using the traditional symbols, S, P, and M.

5. State and prove the Special Rules of all four Figures.

6. Write a note on the Fourth Figure.

7. What is meant by Mood of Syllogism? How are the names of the Moods formed?

8. Construct (*a*) a Barbara syllogism with the terms, good books, lasting possession, worth their price, (*b*) a Camestres syllogism with the terms, carols, sonnets, have a simple structure, (*c*) a Bocardo syllogism with the terms, covenanted subscription, liable to income tax, benefit charity, and (*d*) a Camenes syllogism with the terms, X, Y, and Z.

9. Show that only in the First Figure can there be an A conclusion.

10. EIO is a valid mood in every Figure. IEO is an invalid mood in every Figure. What makes the difference?

11. If the conclusion be substituted for one or other premiss in Barbara, Celarent, Bramantip, Cesare, Camenes, and Camestres, we obtain legitimate pairs of premisses, yielding conclusions, but not in other moods.

12. Which moods admit distributed middle terms in both premisses?

13. Examine the following arguments.

(*a*) The sun is insensible. The Persians worship the sun.
∴ They worship a thing insensible (Port Royal Logic).

(*b*) That which has no parts cannot perish by the dissolution of its parts. The soul has no parts. ∴ It cannot perish by the dissolution of its parts (Port Royal Logic).

(c) He who believes himself to be always in the right in his opinion lays claim to infallibility. You always believe yourself to be right in your opinion (else it would not be your opinion). ∴ You lay claim to infallibility (Whateley).

(d) No evil should be allowed that good may come of it. Punishment is an evil. ∴ Punishment should not be allowed that good may come of it (Whateley).

CHAPTER VI

REDUCTION AND PRINCIPLES OF REASONING

MANY syllogisms can be transposed from one figure into another, as a musical theme can be transposed from one key to another. Aristotle assigned a position of privilege to the first figure (see below, p. 108), and in consequence attention has been concentrated on transposition from the other figures into the first, and with that special problem Reduction is traditionally concerned.

The given syllogism in the second, third, or fourth figure is called the Reducend. The syllogism in the first figure to which it is reduced is called the Reduct. Reducends of most moods transpose directly into their Reducts by the logical processes, already familiar to us, of Conversion, which interchanges subject and predicate, and Metathesis (Mutation), which interchanges the major and minor premisses. This method is called Direct or Ostensive Reduction ; it takes the given material and re-shapes it directly into a syllogism of the first figure. There are, however, two moods—Baroco in the second figure, and Bocardo in the third—which cannot be reduced directly by the processes used for the other moods, because they contain an O premiss. They can be reduced directly, as is shown below, by using Contraposition ; but it is customary to employ in their cases a totally different method, called Indirect Reduction, which reduces *by means of* a first figure syllogism, not *to* a first figure syllogism.

Indirect Reduction is also known as Reduction *per contradictionem* because it employs contradiction, and as Reduction *per impossibile*, because it argues 'If it be possible . . .', and goes on to show that it is not possible. Both these methods and both parts of the aims of traditional Reduction are covered by the following description. *Reduction is the process of expressing the reasoning of a syllogism in the second, third, or fourth figure, by a syllogism in the first figure.*

Direct Reduction is effected with mechanical ease by an intelligent use of the mnemonic hexameters (see p. 97). It will be remembered that the mood name indicates the figure and mood of the syllogism, and that its vowels indicate the quality and quantity of the component propositions. Attention must now be paid to the following points. Most of the consonants (not all) have a meaning. The initial consonant of Reducend and of Reduct is the same. Thus, Festino reduces to Ferio, and Darapti to Darii ; of the medials, *l, r,* and *t* are without significance ; the following table shows the meaning of the others :

c, medial—Indirect Reduction *per contradictionem*.

m, medial—Metathesis, i.e. interchange of premisses.

p, medial or final—*per accidens* Conversion of the preceding proposition.

s, medial or final—simple Conversion of the preceding proposition.

Now apply this technique to an actual case. We are asked to *reduce* the following syllogism :

> No poisons are remedies.
> All antibiotics are remedies.
> ∴ No antibiotics are poisons.

The first step is to find its figure and mood and mood name. It is in the second figure ; its mood is EAE ; its mood name is Cesare. The name Cesare tells us that it can be reduced directly to Celarent by simple conversion of the E premiss. The following method of displaying the successive steps will be found useful:

Reducend		*Reduct*	
C		C	
E No poisons are	*s* No remedies	E No remedies are	
remedies.	are poisons.	poisons.	
S		L	
A All antibiotics		A All antibiotics	
are remedies.		are remedies.	
R		R	
E No antibiotics		E No antibiotics	
are poisons.		are poisons.	
		N	
		T	

Baroco and Bocardo are reduced *directly* to Ferio and Darii, respectively, as follows:

Baroco.   All P is M.
Some S is not M.
∴ Some S is not P.

Contrapose the major and obvert the minor.

No not-M is P.
Some S is not-M.
∴ Some S is not P.

Bocardo.   Some M is not P.
All M is S.
∴ Some S is not P.

Contrapose the major, and then transpose the premisses by metathesis, and contrapose the conclusion.

All M is S.
Some not-P is M.
∴ Some not-P is S.   ∴ Some S is not P.

Indirect Reduction is a complicated, but interesting, process; it can be applied to other moods, but it is chiefly in use for Baroco and Bocardo. Baroco and Bocardo are reduced *indirectly* as follows:

Substitute for the O premiss the contradictory of the conclusion. That yields a valid Barbara syllogism, with a conclusion which contradicts an original premiss given true, and which is therefore false. Our new Barbara syllogism is valid, but has a false conclusion; that can only be because one of its premisses is false. One of its premisses is given true; therefore the other must be false, viz. the contradictory of the original conclusion. Thus by a syllogism in the first figure the contradictory of the original conclusion has been proved false, that is, the original conclusion has been proved true. The method is '*per impossibile*', because the original substitution of the contradictory of the conclusion for the O premiss is equivalent to saying, 'If it be possible, let the conclusion be false; then its contradictory will be true . . . ', and then proceeding to show that its contradictory is false. It is a roundabout, but ingenious method. Example:

Reduce

> All P is M.
> Some S is not M.
> ∴ Some S is not P.

It is a Baroco syllogism; the minor is negative and cannot stand in the first figure. As major (obverted) it cannot stand; for it would be particular. As the *c* indicates, we must contradict the conclusion and substitute the contradictory for the O premiss and proceed indirectly. This yields the valid Barbara syllogism,

All P is M.
All S is P.
∴ All S is M.

This conclusion contradicts the O premiss, given true, and is therefore false. All P is M is given true. Therefore the other premiss, All S is P, is false. Therefore its contradictory, Some S is not P, is true. *Q.E.D.* Bocardo is reduced in a similar way.

I will now take the moods *seriatim*, and will indicate in symbols how each is to be reduced.

Second Figure

Cesare	No P is M	*s*	No M is P
to	All S is M		All S is M
Celarent	No S is P		No S is P

Camestres	All P is M	*m*	No S is M	*s*	No M is S
to	No S is M		All P is M		All P is M
Celarent	No S is P				No P is S

s No S is P

Festino	No P is M	*s*	No M is P
to	Some S is M		Some S is M
Ferio	Some S is not P		Some S is not P

Baroco	All P is M	If possible, let Some S is not P
by	Some S is not M	be false ; then All S is P, its
Barbara	Some S is not P	contradictory, is true. Substi-
		tute it for the O premiss, and
		thus reach the syllogism in
		Barbara (with P as middle term),

All P is M
All S is P
All S is M

This conclusion, All S is M, contradicts the O premiss which is given true. It is therefore false. It has been reached, however, by a valid syllogism. How can it be false? Because while one premiss All P is M is *given* true, the other premiss is only *supposed* true, viz. All S is P. This latter premiss must therefore be false. Since it is false that All S is P, its contradictory, Some S is not P, is true. *Q.E.D.*

Third Figure

Darapti	All M is P		All M is P
to	All M is S	*p*	Some S is M
Darii	Some S is P		Some S is P

Disamis	Some M is P	*m*	All M is S		All M is S
to	All M is S		Some M is P	*s*	Some P is M
Darii	Some S is P				Some P is S
					Some S is P

Datisi	All M is P		All M is P
to	Some M is S	*s*	Some S is M
Darii	Some S is P		Some S is P

Felapton	No M is P		No M is P
to	All M is S	*p*	Some S is M
Ferio	Some S is not P		Some S is not P

Bocardo	Some M is not P	Suppose the conclusion is false,
by	All M is S	then its contradictory, All S is P,
Barbara	Some S is not P	must be true. Substitute it for

the O premiss, and thus reach
the Barbara syllogism, with S
as middle term,

> All S is P
> All M is S
> All M is P

This conclusion, All M is P,
contradicts the O premiss which
is given true. It is therefore
false. It has been reached, however, by a valid syllogism. How
can it be false? Because while
one premiss, All M is S, is *given*
true, the other premiss, All S is
P, is only *supposed* true. This
latter premiss therefore must be
false. Since it is false that All
S is P, its contradictory, Some S
is not P, is true. *Q.E.D.*

Ferison	No M is P		No M is P
to	Some M is S	*s*	Some S is M
Ferio	Some S is not P		Some S is not P

Fourth Figure

Bramantip	All P is M	*m*	All M is S		
by	All M is S		All P is M		
Barbara	Some S is P		All P is S	*p*	Some S is P

Camenes	All P is M	*m*	No M is S		
to	No M is S		All P is M		
Celarent	No S is P		No P is S	*s*	No S is P

Dimaris	Some P is M	*m*	All M is S		
to	All M is S		Some P is M		
Darii	Some S is P		Some P is S	*s*	Some S is P

Fesapo	No P is M	*s*	No M is P
to	All M is S	*p*	Some S is M
Ferio	Some S is not P		Some S is not P

Fresison	No P is M	*s*	No M is P
to	Some M is S	*s*	Some S is M
Ferio	Some S is not P		Some S is not P

Reduction without using the Mood Names

As set out above Reduction tends to become a purely mechanical exercise. To correct this tendency the student, as soon as he has mastered the method, should practise reduction without the aid of the mood names. It can be readily done, if he takes as reducend a simply-worded syllogism, not in the first figure, notes the points in which it differs from the requirements of the first figure as to the position of the middle term and the special rules, and infers from the reducend new premisses that comply with those requirements.

Aristotle's views on Reduction

Aristotle called the first figure " the perfect figure ", and he regarded it as self-evident and as the true type of reasoning. He regarded the second and third figures as imperfect ways of reasoning. He thought that they were not self-evident, and that the best way to prove their validity was to show that their arguments could be reduced to the form of the first figure.[1] He did not accept the fourth figure as independent of the first. Holding these

[1] " All the imperfect syllogisms are made perfect by means of the first figure." *Analytica Priora*, I, 7, 29a.

views he naturally took Reduction very seriously, regarding it as a logical necessity, without which the validity of the second and third figures would remain in doubt. I discuss below the independence of those figures. Here let me say that even if we admit, as I think we have to do, that Aristotle claimed too much for Reduction, that is no reason for going to the other extreme and claiming too little. In any case Reduction remains an important part of Logic. It promotes and tests proficiency in the syllogistic system, and rounds off the doctrine of inference with a sustained and elegant piece of reasoning that suggests the unity of reason, as geometry suggests the unity of space.

In the first place, then, there is no denying that the first figure has advantages over the others. In it alone can an A conclusion be drawn; in it alone can conclusions in all four types (A, E, I, O) be drawn; and owing to the placing of its terms first figure arguments are, as a rule, clear to follow and easy to accept. The first figure is the superior figure, and its universal moods (Barbara and Celarent) often possess the cogency associated with scientific demonstrations. To admit that superiority, however, is not to admit that there is any positive imperfection in the second and third figures. They stand on their own feet and are valid in their own right. They have their own special uses and represent actual movements of the mind.

The fourth figure is not independent, and it has no special use. Arguments in it are, as a rule, awkward and unnatural. With these points in mind we will now consider *seriatim* concrete examples of argument in the second, third, and fourth figures.

Second Figure Inference

The second figure is distinguished outwardly by being always in the negative mood, and by the position of the middle term as predicate of both premisses. Is there in it a distinctive mode of inference to match these distinctive outward characters ? Take a normal Cesare syllogism and compare it with its reduct, Celarent.

Cesare	*Celarent*
No brown trout are migrant fish.	No migrant fish are brown trout.
All sea trout are migrant fish.	All sea trout are migrant fish.
∴ No sea trout are brown trout.	∴ No sea trout are brown trout.

On Aristotle's view the Celarent syllogism is superior to its Cesare equivalent, and possesses a higher degree of cogency, because it exemplifies more clearly the principle (as he saw it) of syllogistic reasoning. Anyone in doubt about the validity of the Cesare syllogism ought, on the Aristotelian view, to ' validate ' it by converting its major and thus reducing the syllogism to Celarent. Now when you see the two examples side by side, it is hard to believe that Aristotle is right in this case ; for here the conversion of the major is no improvement, but the reverse. It is more natural to deny that brown trout are migrants than to deny that migrants are brown trout. The Cesare form is perfectly natural and convincing and its inference is distinctive. We argue in effect that if sea trout were brown trout, they would stay in their river, and would not go down to the sea ; but they do go down to the sea. *We perceive the validity of the conclusion by perceiving that its contradictory is inconsistent with given fact.* It is a true and independent movement of thought, characteristic of inference in the second figure. What holds of Cesare holds of the other moods of the second figure. Of course, we may happen on a particular syllogism in the second figure that would go more naturally in the first figure; but such 'stray sheep' prove nothing. We must judge each figure by its characteristic movement.

Third Figure Inference

The third figure is distinguished outwardly by the position of the middle term as subject of both premisses, and by the particularity of all its conclusions. It is known as the 'Inductive figure', because its conclusions, being particular, furnish material for induction (see below, p. 172). Has it a distinctive mode of inference? Take a syllogism in Datisi, and compare it with its reduct, Darii.

Datisi	*Darii*
All men are mortal.	All men are mortal.
Some men are philosophers.	Some philosophers are men.
∴ Some philosophers are mortal.	∴ Some philosophers are mortal.

Here too it is hard to accept Aristotle's view. Do you find the Datisi argument any less clear than the Darii? Could any doubts about the former be removed by transposing to the latter? The shoe is on the other foot. It is distinctly more natural to say 'Some men are philosophers' than to say 'Some philosophers are men.' The affirmative moods of the third figure bring together two general terms (e.g. *philosophers* and *mortal*) by means of the middle term (e.g. *men*). The negative moods of the third figure exclude two general terms, the one from the other, by means of the middle term. *The third figure in*

all its moods shows us the validity of its conclusions by re-
minding us of the particular instances that confirm its truth.
' Some philosophers are mortal.' Yes, Plato, Aristotle,
Locke, Berkeley, Kant and Hegel. They all exemplified
the truth of the conclusion. In the third figure these
confirmatory instances readily come to mind. Aristotle
himself mentioned this feature of third figure inference;
he called it ' Exposition ', and accepted it as a mode
of validation, a second-best (for him) alternative to reduction. We must go further here than Aristotle, and
must regard this ' expository ' feature of the third figure,
as establishing it as an independent mode of inference,
with a special use and a distinctive movement of thought,
valid in its own right.

Fourth Figure Inference

The fourth figure is distinguished outwardly by the fact
that in it both extremes occupy different positions in premiss and conclusion. It has no special use; it is dependent on other figures, and its syllogisms rarely exhibit a
natural movement of thought. Its moods fall into two
groups. In the *m* group (Bramantip, Camenes, and
Dimaris) the premisses are in an unnatural order; restore
the natural order by metathesis, and the inference proceeds
naturally in the first figure. The other two moods (Fesapo
and Fresison) do not admit metathesis. For our purpose
they may be treated as one; for what goes for the universal
minor goes also for the particular minor. Take this
Fesapo syllogism:

> No voters are aliens.
> All aliens are industrious.
> ∴ Some industrious people are not voters.

As it stands the validity of the inference is not obvious; it is valid, but one has to refer to the rules to be sure. The syllogism lacks clarity; for the terms of its major premiss are in an unnatural order. Three transpositions are possible: (*a*) We can convert the minor, and transpose into the second figure (Festino), (*b*) We can convert both premisses, and transpose into the first figure (Ferio), (*c*) We can convert the major only, and transpose into the third figure (Felapton). The Festino form leaves the awkward major unconverted. The Ferio transposition is better; but the Felapton form is best; for it involves the least change, and the characteristic third figure movement of thought appears in the Felapton form:

No aliens are voters.
All aliens are industrious.
∴ Some industrious people are not voters.

Aristotle's Dictum

Aristotle's *Dictum de omni et de nullo* is a formula to express the principle of syllogistic reasoning. It has come down to us in several forms, of which the shortest is that given by Zabarella,[1] *What is predicated about any whole is predicated about any part of that whole.* That Aristotle formulated and used some such principle, and connected it in a special way with the first figure is certain; but as we do not know for certain the form in which he expressed it, nor the exact use he made of it, several disputed points about it must be left unsettled.

The principal passage about it in Aristotle's extant works

[1] Count Jacopo Zabarella, Italian philosopher and logician, *c.* 1533–89.

is the following. "That one term should be included in another as in a whole is the same as for the other to be predicated of all of the first. And we say that one term is predicated of all of another, whenever no instance of the subject can be found of which the other term cannot be asserted; ' to be predicated of none ' must be understood in the same way." [1] It is a highly compressed passage. The word *predicated* covers both affirmation and denial, and that explains the full title of the *Dictum*. It is *de omni et de nullo*, because it is about *all* and *none*, i.e. it is about the universal affirmative (A) and about the universal negative (E). To bring out the full meaning of the *Dictum* it should be expanded into two statements, viz. :

Whatever is affirmed of any whole is affirmed of any part of that whole. Whatever is denied of any whole is denied of any part of that whole.

The *Dictum de omni* (universal affirmative) is clearly exemplified in the Barbara syllogism, and likewise the *Dictum de nullo* (universal negative) in the Celarent syllogism. For instance, take the following Barbara :

All men are mortal.
All pigmies are men.
∴ All pigmies are mortal.

Mortal, affirmed of the whole *man-kind*, is clearly affirmed of its part *pigmy-kind*. The cogency of the argument leaps to the eye; one almost *sees* its validity. The same holds of the universal negative in the first figure. Take for instance, the following Celarent :

No fresh-water fish attain a great size rapidly.
All brown trout are fresh-water fish.
∴ No brown trout attain a great size rapidly.

[1] *Analytica Priora*, I, 1, 24b.

Rapid growth, denied of all fresh-water fish, is *eo ipso* denied of a section of that group, namely brown trout. In all such cases the visual imagery of inclusion and exclusion greatly assists the inference.

Whether Aristotle regarded the *Dictum* as the principle of *all* syllogistic reasoning, and if so, whether he was right to do so, are matters in dispute. Logicians are also not agreed as to the sense in which ' whole and part ' in the *Dictum* are to be understood. Do the terms apply only to denotation and extension, or to connotation as well? Again, does the clarity attaching to the Barbara and Celarent syllogisms trace to the nature of the first figure, or to the universality of the moods or to the combination of both? However these questions are answered, Aristotle's *Dictum* retains its historic interest and importance as an attempt to penetrate into the heart of reasoning and solve the problem of inference as a whole.

The value of the Syllogism

The syllogism has long been a target for criticism. It has been cried up and cried down unduly. Extravagant claims for it have been countered by an undeserved depreciation. ' All reasoning is syllogistic ', some have said, claiming that any valid argument ought to be expressible in syllogistic form. " Everything is a syllogism ", a philosopher once said in a dialectical flight. Backwards and forwards the pendulum has swung. Francis Bacon (see below, p. 176) attacked the syllogism, and the attack has often been repeated since his day. Much of this criticism is misdirected; it should be aimed, not at the syllogism itself, but at excessive claims made for it by its undiscerning champions. The syllogism in itself is a sound and useful instrument of reasoning, and most of its critics are fairly met by the frank admission that there are other ways of reasoning, and that not all arguments will go into syllogistic form.

One specific charge against the syllogism must now be considered at some length. It is an old criticism, urged in antiquity; and it received new force last century when Mill wrote, " It must be granted that in every syllogism, considered as an argument to prove the conclusion, there is a *petitio principii*." [1] If this charge were admitted in full, the value of syllogistic studies would be seriously reduced, though, as Mill is at pains to point out, the syllogism would still possess value as a register of knowledge gained. In my view the charge ought not to be admitted in full, nor rejected out of hand. The criticism should force us to examine our syllogisms, and distinguish those that are open to this charge from those that are not.

In the syllogism,

> All men are mortal.
> Socrates is a man.
> ∴ Socrates is mortal,

there is a *petitio principii*, says Mill; that is, we beg the question, and assume what we set out to prove. Is Socrates mortal? That is the Question. We assume that he is mortal when we say ' All men are mortal '; for if *he* were not mortal, that major premiss would not be true. In Mill's words, " We cannot be assured of the mortality of all men, unless we are already certain of the mortality of every individual man."

I have raised the question in Mill's words, because the

---

[1] J. S. Mill, *A System of Logic*, Book II, iii, 3.

discussion owes much to his presentation of the case; and those who wish to go further into the question should read what he has to say about it. But there is some doubt as to the details of his teaching, and it is not quite certain what he meant by his qualification ' considered as an argument to prove the conclusion'. We shall therefore leave Mill out of it. Let us simply consider whether the syllogism does necessarily ' beg the question', and if so, whether the syllogism loses much in value.

Petitio Principii or ' Begging the Question' (see below, p. 167) is the fallacy of assuming what you pretend to prove, or ought to prove. As a charge against the syllogism it amounts to saying that we put into the premisses what we intend to take out in the conclusion, that therefore the argument of every syllogism ends where it began, like the circumference of a circle, and registers no advance from the known to the unknown. The charge in a nutshell is that the syllogism is circular, i.e. that it ' goes round in circles'. In discussing the question we ought to begin by distinguishing between syllogism and syllogism; we ought not to ' lump' them all together. It is a case in which we cannot go by the form of the syllogism alone, and it does not follow that because some syllogisms are circular, all are. Syllogisms in symbols are of no use here; we must study the content, and then we find that some syllogisms are circular, some rectilinear, and some doubtful. It is also important to distinguish between collective knowledge, say the knowledge represented by an encyclopedia, and personal knowledge, your knowledge and mine. A conclusion of a syllogism may represent no advance in collective knowledge, and yet may be a very significant advance in personal knowledge. ' Socrates is mortal' is a truism to us; but it meant a step forward in knowledge to young Socrates himself long ago. Men are learners, and there is always more for us to learn. We cannot take out of a pair of premisses what is not there ; but we can take out, and often do take out, *what we did not put there*. The personal aspect of syllogizing must not be overlooked. Syllogisms have no tongues ; they cannot argue or infer or go round in circles. The man who syllogizes does these things. When we discuss whether or not the syllogism is circular, we are really discussing whether we ourselves are begging the question, when we syllogize ; and that way of putting the problem often makes a difference to the answer. If, for instance, I were asked whether I assume the mortality of Socrates when I assert that all men are mortal, I should reply, No. So far as I can judge the workings of my own mind, I do not beg that question. Others may do so ; each man must speak for himself. ' All men are mortal ' —I frame and assert that premiss without any thought, good, bad, or indifferent, of Socrates or of any other individual. In other syllogisms I might beg the question, but not in this case. If by ' All men are mortal ' you mean that all men up to date have died, then of course you cannot know its truth without first knowing that Socrates has died. But that is not what *I* mean by the major premiss. To make it mean merely that all men up to date have died seems to me unnatural. It is like saying that St. Paul's ' All have sinned . . .' means ' All men up to date have sinned . . .' St. Paul did not mean it so, and the average reader would not take it so. The All in ' All men are mortal ' and in ' All have sinned ' is not said of an arithmetical aggregate, but of the whole of a kind ; and both predicates in their natural meaning are qualities or attributes of our common humanity, essential parts of the

connotation of the term *man*. The circularity, or otherwise, of this particular syllogism turns, it seems to me, on
the question of denotation or connotation. Those who
understand the 'All men are mortal' solely in terms of
denotation, would by implication include Socrates in it,
and the syllogism to them would be circular. But those
who understand it primarily in terms of connotation, as
seems more natural, would take it to mean that mortality
is a universal attribute of mankind, and on learning from
the minor premiss that Socrates is a man, they would go
on in a straight line to infer that he is mortal.

Now consider a very homely syllogism:

All College societies are open to men and women.
Chess clubs are College societies.
∴ Chess clubs are open to men and women.

Here thought is moving within the narrow field of College
regulations. All recognized College societies are to be
open to students of both sexes, and chess clubs are to
rank as College societies. These rules are not written
across the sky; they are just matters of College policy,
alterable by a stroke of the pen. The Governing Body
could remove chess clubs from the list of College societies,
and then the conclusion would not be true. As things
are, it is given true, and that must be because 'All College
societies' really means 'All the College societies on the
official list, including chess clubs.' The Officers of the
College might well regard that syllogism as circular.
They would be only taking out of it what they themselves
put in, and would not be advancing from the known to the
unknown. The Freshman, however, might extend his
knowledge of College regulations from the syllogism; if
so it would not be circular to him.

E

A scientific syllogism such as the following, has a deeper character.

All *Ranunculi bulbosi* have drooping sepals.
This flower is a *Ranunculus bulbosus*.
∴ It has drooping sepals.

This syllogism represents a hard-won insight into the structure of plant life and a long development of scientific method to express and systematize the facts. Buttercups are buttercups ; but some have bulbs and some have creeping runners, and those with bulbs have drooping sepals, and those with creeping runners have spreading sepals. It is one of many correlations within the *genus* that goes to build scientific knowledge. Botanists teach from it without recourse to particular observation. If we regard the major premiss as merely a shorthand statement about the sepals of a host of individual buttercups, past, present, and to be, its truth would need checking in every instance, and the syllogism as a basis of inference would be circular. But that interpretation does less than justice to the biological knowledge involved in the major premiss. Certainly in the mouth of a botanist the major premiss would be a true universal, and not merely an enumerative statement about an aggregate of specimens of buttercup. If a trained botanist used the syllogism in question, one would expect it to be to him rectilinear, and not circular.

Finally a student of this question should weigh the evidence of what might be called ' a syllogism in the making '. If we confine our attention to completed, ' ready-made ' syllogisms, we are apt to regard them as circular, because we forget the actual progress in knowledge they represent. But if it is the case that we sometimes do *acquire* truth syllogistically, and not merely register it in a syllogism, if we first learn one true premiss, and then after an interval a second true premiss, and if on putting the two premisses together, we infer a true conclusion, completely unexpected at the outset, if in fact we sometimes *learn* a truth by building a syllogism, then it becomes impossible to write off *all* syllogisms as circular, without any advance from the known to the unknown.

Take the case of a young philosopher who is seriously interested in conduct and the science of ethics. One Michaelmas term, we will suppose, he makes an intensive study of the pleasure-motive. Were the Epicureans right about it, or the Stoics? Ought man to seek pleasure, or despise it, or ignore it, or be neutral towards it? Is hedonism ethical? With such questions in mind our young philosopher gets down to it. He compares pleasure with pleasure, noting the transience of some pleasures and the relative permanence of others; he weighs the satisfaction of pleasure over against the prior want and the subsequent regret. The paradox of hedonism impresses him; if you want to *get* pleasure, *forget* it. If pleasure is so mixed with pain, can it be really part of the happy life? He then turns from pleasure in the abstract to concrete pleasures. Food and drink, family life, social life, fresh air and exercise, leisure and hobbies, conversation, music and the merry heart, art, learning and piety, the love of God and man—how could anyone be really happy without some at least of these pleasant things? Admitting that there are apparent pleasures that issue in pain and that abstract pleasure is a phantom, still it would seem that concrete pleasures must form part of concrete human happiness. And so our young moralist concluded when he summarized the results of his Michaelmas research in the general statement, 'All true pleasures conduce to happiness.'

Now suppose in the next Hilary term he approached the problem of conduct from a different angle, and examined the points at issue between altruism and egoism, and the eternal conflict between duty and self-interest. He would be forced to consider the contrast between higher and lower pleasures, between real and apparent pleasures, and the connection between unselfishness and enlightened self-interest. His research along those lines might well culminate in the principle, ' All unselfish acts are true pleasures.' If that happened—and such things do happen in the higher work of mind—automatically a syllogistic link has been established between his two terms' work. Michaelmas term yielded the major premiss, the next Hilary term yielded the minor premiss. No thinking man could refuse to put this ' two and two ' together, and draw the conclusion :

> All true pleasures conduce to happiness.
> All unselfish acts are true pleasures.
> ∴ All unselfish acts conduce to happiness.

It is a valid syllogism enshrining an important truth. Viewed as a ' syllogism in the making ' it is not circular ; to the young learner who thought it out, it is a rectilinear argument, advancing from the known to the unknown.

Is the syllogism circular ? It is an instructive question, and it deserves a discriminating answer. Undoubtedly there are circular syllogisms, and how they may be known has been pointed out above, and the value of such syllogisms lies principally in their power to end disputes and cut short debates by presenting a record and register of agreed truth and accepted principle. Then, too, there are doubtful cases and border-line cases ; there are syllogisms that are circular to one man, and not to another ;

occupation, time of life, and maturity of judgment affect the way in which premisses are stated and conclusions drawn. But undoubtedly there are, it seems to me, syllogisms that are not circular, in which there is a valid inference, and an advance from the known to the previously unknown. Such syllogisms extend the knowledge of the individual, and probably therefore in the long run extend collective knowledge.

The syllogism in general has value; it has stood the test of time; in studying its technique we are studying a form of discursive thinking, which is in actual use, and has made a contribution to human knowledge. We use syllogistic reasoning even when we do not stop to put our argument into syllogistic form. We use the syllogism unconsciously; we do well to learn to use it consciously. In mastering its mechanism and learning the drill we are alerted to many dangers that attend other sorts of reasoning as well. Good art-forms foster good taste all round; and good syllogizing helps to make good reasoners; for the syllogism is a standardized pattern of right reasoning, easily studied and always at hand; it is non-specialized, and it well suits the more important affairs of the human spirit, and the graver arguments in which the mind of man engages.

The 'Laws of Thought' [1]

The phrase the 'Laws of Thought' refers traditionally to three rules of right thinking which from Aristotle's day

---

[1] These 'Laws' can be studied under Immediate Inference, with reference to Contradiction and Contrariety; but a discussion of them is not necessary there, and they belong more naturally to an advanced stage. For fuller treatment see J. N. Keynes, *Formal Logic*, 4th ed., London, 1928, Appendix B.

have been recognized as occupying a position of fundamental importance. They are, the Law of Identity, the Law of Contradiction, and the Law of the Excluded Middle. The term *Law* is metaphorical, as in the phrase 'Laws of Nature'; but the Laws of Thought and the Laws of Nature are *Laws* in rather different senses. The Laws of Thought are mainly *normative*, while the Laws of Nature are mainly *descriptive*. The Laws of Nature describe the ways in which Nature behaves; they may regulate our behaviour *towards* Nature; but they do not regulate the behaviour *of* Nature. The Laws of Thought to some extent describe the ways in which we think; but their chief purpose is to regulate and control our thinking by setting up a *norm*, i.e. an example and standard, of right thinking. Human thinking follows the pattern of being, and naturally the Laws of Thought often take on the aspect of Laws of Being; but for Logic they are primarily Axioms of Consistent Thinking. They apply both to terms and to propositions, but in connection with propositions their value is most clearly seen. All three Laws are closely related. Contradiction is the negative side of Identity, and finds its complement and completion in the Exclusion of the Middle.

The Law of Identity is expressed in the formula, A is A. Eggs are eggs, and must be called so. Things are what they are, and so far as in us lies, the terms in which we speak of them must be used with a clear, defined, and fixed meaning. Serious discourse with folk who do not bother, or do not care, to fix the meaning of their terms, or who vary their meaning without notice, is impossible.

The Law of Contradiction is expressed in the formula, A is not not-A, or A is not both B and not-B. Contradiction puts negatively what Identity puts positively. Eggs are eggs. Eggs are not not-eggs. The same rose cannot be both red and not-red. If someone urges that one part of the same rose might be red, and another part not-red, or that the rose which is red today may be faded and grey tomorrow, we have only to make the Law more explicit by adding 'in respect of the same part', or 'at the same time'. Two contradictory propositions cannot both be true.

The Law of the Excluded Middle adds that they cannot both be false. It is expressed in the formula, A is either B or not-B. *Middle* has nothing to do with the middle term of the syllogism; it is just a convenient name for a supposed mid-way position. There is no 'half-way house', as we say, between B and not-B, and therefore 'A is B' and 'A is not-B' cannot both be false. There is a *Middle* between *wise* and *foolish*, e.g. *imprudent*; and so 'Jones is wise' and 'Jones is foolish' could both be false. Jones might be neither wise nor foolish, but imprudent. That *Middle* is not excluded. There is no *Middle* between *wise* and *not-wise*. 'Smith is wise' and 'Smith is not-wise' cannot both be false. If he is not one, he is the other.

Questions and Exercises on Chapter VI

1. Distinguish direct reduction from indirect. Which moods cannot be reduced directly by the ordinary methods?

2. Show how to reduce (*a*) with the mood names, and (*b*) without them, in concrete terms.

3. Invent a Baroco syllogism, and reduce it.

4. Using symbols as terms, take syllogisms in Cesare, Darapti, and Camenes, and reduce them.

5. How did Aristotle view the problem of reduction? Examine his view.

6. State the special uses (if any) of each of the our figures. Indicate their peculiarities and characteristics, external and internal, and discuss the question of their validation.

7. What is Aristotle's *Dictum*? Discuss the details of it, and estimate its worth.

8. Discuss the present-day value of the syllogism, with special reference to Mill's criticisms.

9. Specify the traditional 'Laws of Thought'; show the relation between them, and explain their force and meaning and application.

CHAPTER VII

THE CATEGORIES AND PREDICABLES.
GENUS, SPECIES, AND CLASS. DIAGRAMS

The Categories and Predicables

Both these Aristotelian doctrines have deeply influenced thought. Both concern predicates. *Category* is a Greek word for *predicate*, and the doctrine of the Categories treats predicates as they are in themselves. The doctrine of the Predicables treats predicates in their varying relations to the subject of the proposition.

The Ten Categories

Here is Aristotle's list, with examples:

Substance	. .	man, horse, stone
Quantity	. .	large, small
Quality	. .	good, bad, blue, wet
Relation	. .	alike, different, near, far, larger
Place	. .	here, there, in London, in Dublin
Time	. .	now, then, never, A.D. 1066
Situation	. .	sitting, standing, upside down
State	. .	healthy, wet through, distressed
Action	. .	swimming, writing, planning
Passion	. .	being beaten, bleeding (e.g. a bleeding nose; medical 'bleeding' would be Action)

The Categories, as conceived by Aristotle, were types of predicates and types of being. They answer the questions, What is this predicate in itself? What is this being in itself? The two questions amount to much the same

thing; for a predicate must have some sort of being, or
it would not be said of a subject. The predicate is what
its subject is; but when we take examples, we soon find
that the word 'is' has different aspects and represents
different types of being. The fish is a trout. The fish is
four pounds. The fish is fresh. The fish is smaller. The
fish is in the net. The fish is in the month of June. The
fish is tailing. The fish is tiring. The fish is taking the fly.
The fish is netted. These ten statements about the one
subject all make sense; but they all differ in character.
The first stands out above the rest, and provides the peg,
as it were, on which the others hang. The fish is a four-
pound trout, a fresh trout, a smaller trout, etc. Being
a trout it is (as we say) a *thing* that can have these and the
other predicates. To be a *thing* is to be a *substance* in
technical language. *Substance* is the first and most important category; it means *that which exists in itself*, and all
the other categories may be viewed as ways in which substances exist. There is nothing that exists, in Aristotle's
view, that cannot be brought under one or other of the
ten categories. If the predicate is not a substance, then
it must be a quantity, a quality, a time, a place or state,
etc.; one or other of them must be predicable of everything; they are 'ultimates'; we cannot go behind them;
a time is not a place or a state, nor is a quantity a quality.

Aristotle's list of categories is open to criticism, and
attempts have been made, notably by Kant and Mill, to
improve on it; but it is still the best list available for
general purposes. There is some overlapping in it;
quality and *state* tend to run into one another, and so do
place and *situation*; there may be some omissions from the
list; and it is extremely hard to say what Substance is,
and what is, and is not, a substance; but by and large

Aristotle's doctrine of the Categories has great value still; it helps us to classify our predicates, and to understand fundamental features of discourse and of the mysterious world in which and of which we discourse.

The Predicables

Under *Categories* terms were considered as standing by themselves out of construction.   Under Predicables predicates are to be considered standing in construction in relation to their subjects.

> Man is animal.
> Man is rational.
> Man is temperamental.

The three propositions have the same outward form; but they differ in force and scope, because their predicates are related to their subjects in very different ways. *Animal* is predicable of *man* in one way; *rational* is predicable of *man* in a very different way. Aristotle recognized five Heads of Predicables, Definition, *Genus, Differentia*, Property, Accident.[1] These technical terms are household words; they are enshrined in homely proverbs and maxims, as well as in axioms and scientific principles. They show how deeply Aristotle penetrated into the nature of discourse, and what an abiding influence his Logic has been, and is, on the thought and speech of educated and uneducated alike.

Definition (see above, p. 27) is a statement of the essence of anything. *Genus* (see below, p. 131) is part of

---

[1] *Topica*, I, 4, 101b, 17–25. Porphyry (A.D. 233–*c.* 304), Greek philosopher, whose *Isagoge* (i.e. Introduction to Aristotle's Categories) was used as a manual of Logic in the middle ages, substituted *Species* for *Definition*—a departure from the original plan of the doctrine.

the essence of a thing, namely that part which can be predicated also of other things, differing from it in kind. *Differentia*, too, is part of the essence of a thing, but is that part which distinguishes it from other *species* of its *genus*.

Property is a more difficult notion and somewhat fluid. Aristotle meant it to be (as the name shows) an attribute proper and peculiar to the Subject, but not part of its essence. *We* often speak of ' essential properties '. Accident covers all other attributes. An Accident is an attribute which may, or may not, belong to the subject ; e.g. Socrates is *in the Piraeus*.

As stated above, a good definition defines *per genus et differentiam*. ' Man is a rational animal ' is a good definition ; it states the *genus animal* that man shares with horses and cattle, etc., at the same time specifying the differentia *rational* that marks him off from other species of animal. But is man not also differentiated by laughter, tears, and speech ? It is hard to find a fully satisfactory answer. Laughter, tears, and speech are prized privileges of man, bound up with rationality. They are certainly not accidental ; but they seem to fall short of essence. He may not be able to speak or laugh or cry ; but ' A man's a man for a' that '. If Property is to be that which borders on essence, yet falls short, we may fairly class laughter and tears and speech as Properties of man.

The Five Predicables could be illustrated from the being and nature of *Man* as follows :

Definition of Man .	Rational animal
His *Genus* . . .	Animal
His *Differentia* . .	Rational
His Properties . .	Laughter, tears, speech
His Accidents . .	Cooking food, living for seventy years

Commensurability

The Predicables can be grouped in two ways; above we put together Definition, *Genus* and *Differentia* as dealing with essence, and over against those three stand Property and Accident. In respect of Commensurability they fall into a different grouping.

Subject and predicate are said to be Commensurate, when the extension of both terms is identical; that is, when either term can be said of everything whereof the other term is said. This can happen only when the predicate is a Definition or a Property. Definition and Property therefore form one group. 'Man is a rational animal'; subject and predicate are commensurate, because the extension of *Man* and of *rational animal* coincide. 'Man can laugh'; laughter is his Property; no other animal can laugh; *Man* and *can laugh* are Commensurate. Not so with *Genus*, *Differentia*, and Accident; they are not Commensurate. 'Man is an animal'; *animal* is his *Genus*; but there are many other animals, besides man. 'Man is rational'; reason differentiates man from all other animals, but not from all other beings, so far as we know. God, *ex hypothesi*, is rational, and the Intelligences or angelic beings are assumed to be rational. 'Man lives for seventy years'; so do elephants and carp. Thus where *Genus*, *Differentia*, and Accident are predicated, subject and predicate are not commensurate.

Classification. Genus and Species[1]

Genus, *species*, group, family, class—these words are

---

[1] For the biological information I am indebted to my colleague, Professor D. A. Webb

often used indiscriminately in ordinary life for any sort of collection of individuals ; but some of them, especially *genus* and *species*, have a long history, and there are certain differences and distinctions which ought to be observed by all who value precision, where precision is in place.

The first distinction is that between the natural class and the artificial class. The natural class is more properly called the kind or the *genus* ; it is there whether we classify or not ; like man*kind*, or animal-*kind*, it is something that shows in every individual man or animal, a pattern of being that makes the individual, man or animal, what it is. The artificial class is made by the act of classing, and does not mould the members of the class, nor make them what they are. If there is a large heap of cobblestones on the road, and the contractor shovels half to the right of the road and half to the left, he has made a classification of sorts ; class A is on the right, and class B is on the left ; but you could transfer cobbles from the one pile to the other without affecting the classes. Class A and Class B are just aggregates in such a case. On the other hand, the natural class or *genus* is not a mere aggregate or a bare collection. The *genus* in Logic is not properly a class at all. The *genus* is exemplified in the members of the *genus* ; they display the internal pattern and structure of the *genus*. The class is not exemplified in the members of the class ; at best they wear the external livery of the class. Smith minor is in Class III. Class III is little more than an aggregate of boys within certain limits of age and intelligence. Smith minor could scarcely be said to exemplify Class III ; at any rate he does not exemplify that class as he exemplifies his *genus*, *human boy*. He would be the same Smith minor in Class II, or almost the same.

The *genus* of anything, says Joseph (*op. cit.*, p. 84) is

" a scheme which it realizes, an unity connecting it with things different from itself ".

In Logic *genus* and *species* are relative terms. *Animal* is *genus* ; *man* is *species*. *Man* is *genus* ; *Frenchman* is *species*. *Frenchman* is *genus* ; *Parisian* is *species* ; and no doubt there are *species* of the *genus Parisian*. That elastic system meets most of the requirements of Logic, and is the method followed, for the most part, in the random classifications of ordinary life. It would not suit the present-day requirements of the sciences, which need more terms than *genus* and *species*, and a rigid system of a hierarchical pattern. Plants and animals are classified in the same way, and biological method, while retaining *genus* and *species* and assigning them definite places, has brought in other group-terms (see p. 137) and arranged all in the form of a hierarchy.

In Logic we must always think of the connotation of terms as well as of their denotation ; we pass in thought from *Frenchman* to *man*, not by counting heads, but by abstracting qualities and attributes. Omit from the term *Frenchman* white, witty, mercurial, and inhabitant of France, and we have gone a long way towards forming the *genus man*, of which Frenchman is a *species*. When two common terms are so related that the connotation of the one includes the connotation of the other, the term with the larger connotation is called the Species, and the term with the smaller connotation is called the Genus.

Aristotle[1] defined *genus* as " what is predicated in the category of essence of a number of things exhibiting differences in kind ". That is a compressed way of saying that *genus* is that part of the essential meaning of a term which is predicated also of other *species*. Thus *man* is the

[1] *Topica*, I, 5 102a.

genus of *Frenchman*, not because it has a wider extension, but because *manhood*, our common humanity, is what the *species* Frenchman, Englishman, etc., have in common. Similarly animal is the *genus* of man, not because there are more animals and more kinds of animals than men and kinds of men, but because *animal* is what man shares with horses and cattle, etc.

As far back as Plato the *genus* has been spoken of as 'higher' than the *species*. 'Higher' is a mere metaphor, based, it would seem, on the fact that the higher we climb the more extension we see. 'Up and down' do not apply literally to *genus* and *species*; nor is the *genus* necessarily higher in the scale of values than the *species*. The upper limit of the abstracting process is known as the *Genus Summum*, and its lower limit as the *Species Infima*. Both

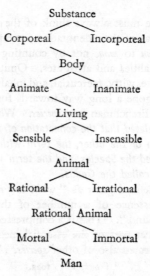

Substance

Corporeal   Incorporeal

Body

Animate   Inanimate

Living

Sensible   Insensible

Animal

Rational   Irrational

Rational Animal

Mortal   Immortal

Man

limits are only ideal resting-places for the mind. The imaginary line joining the *Genus Summum* to the *Species Infima*, and passing through the intermediate *genera* and *species* has been called a Predicamental Line. Such a line is the *Arbor Porphyriana*, a historic classification which ' places ' man in the scale of being by the method of logical dichotomy (see facing page).

Turning to more recent times, let us view these ancient terms in the light of the modern method.

Plant Biology and Modern Hierarchical Classification

I hold in my hand a broad bean. I see and touch it ; I could cook and eat it. There are countless millions more like it, and of course it has no proper name ; but to single it out and mark it off from other beans we will call it ' B.B.'. If I only want to look at it and admire its colours or eat it, the question of classification does not arise ; it is just ' B.B.', one of many similar objects ; but as soon as I want to *know* about it, and to make it a spring-board for further knowing, classification becomes necessary. I lose interest in the individuality of ' B.B.'. In thought I abstract its place, time, age, weight, price, and provenance, and all else about it that is not relevant to general knowledge. What I now need to know is summed up in the botanical statement that ' B.B.' is a seed of *Vicia faba*, or, as the logician would be inclined to say, an instance of *Vicia faba*. *Vicia faba* is its name to botanists the world over. That name represents and assists in perpetuating a vast apparatus of knowledge, methodically acquired, not a little of it based on the logic of *genus* and *species*. For *Vicia* is the *genus* of ' B.B.', and *faba* is its *species*. There are many other *species* in the *genus*, amongst them *Vicia sepium*, the common vetch that runs in our hedgerows, and *Vicia cracca*, the tufted vetch. Each species has its *differentia*, its distinctive character or peculiarity. Each *species* has something in common with all the other *species* of *Vicia*, and that ' something common ' is the *genus*, i.e. the connotation of the term *Vicia*. This *genus* is far more than a *name* ; it does more than designate a collection of individual plants ; it designates and *is* the common fund of shared characters, which mark all members of the *genus*, *Vicia*, as a family likeness, physical or mental, marks all members of a human family.

For many centuries the botanist worked with a hand-list of *genera*. Up to about the year 1500 the accepted kinds of plants, each with a noun-name, *Ranunculus* (buttercup), *Ulex* (furze), *Erica* (heath), etc., were listed in alphabetical order ; but with the growth of knowledge the first simple card-index system became totally inadequate, and *that* in two directions ; on the one hand, as a result of observation and travel, there was an enormous increase in the number of the known kinds and of the varieties known to occur under each kind ; and on the other hand, there was an even more important advance in scientific knowledge of the differentiating characters of the kinds, their subtlety, complexity, and constancy. Botany became Plant Biology. Naturalists realized that the *kind* was a complex affair, covering several correlated varieties of kinds, such as the varieties of buttercup, mentioned above, p. 120, in which the shape of the sepal is correlated with the method of propagation. A mere hand-list of *genera* in which all buttercups are lumped as *Ranunculi* became totally inadequate to the new knowledge, and the first step to meet the situation was to add the adjective. The noun *Ranunculus* remained as the *genus*, and under it were grouped its *species*, *Ranunculus bulbosus*, *Ranunculus repens*, *Ranunculus alpestris*, etc., each marked by an adjective that expressed its differentiating character.

In this system, established in the eighteenth century and still the basis of botanical classification, the *species* (noun and adjective) has taken the place of the original *genus* (noun), and become the ultimate fact, the ' kind ' mentioned in the Mosaic account of creation, the smallest class in which correlated variation was regular and predictable. Darwin's title, *The Origin of Species*, reflects this usage, and the *species* still has a privileged position and is regarded as more natural and less conventional than the *genus*. The name *genus* in biology is now little more than a convenient term for the aggregate of the species.

When the flora of America and the East was taken into account, the material to be classified became so vast that a much more elaborate system of classifying was called for, and the following hierarchy of groups, though in parts arbitrary, is fixed by usage and international convention : *Phylum*, *Class*, *Sub-class*, *Order*, *Family*, *Genus*, *Species*. Fully classified in accordance with this system, the broad bean (' B.B.') from which we started this analysis would have the following class-pedigree :

			Differentia
Phylum	.	Spermatophyta	Seed-plants (distinct from ferns, mosses, etc.)
Class	.	Angiospermae	Flowering plants (distinct from Conifers, etc.)
Sub-class	.	Dicotyledones	Seedlings with two leaves
Order	.	Leguminosae	Possessing a pod
Family	.	Papilionaceae	Flowers like butterflies
Genus	.	Vicia	Style hairy, leaflets numerous, etc.
Species	.	Vicia faba	Large seed, woolly lining to pod, etc.

When one reflects on the foregoing classification of a common broad bean from the garden, one sees something of the complexity of nature, of her inexhaustible variety, shot through and through with order and design. Any of these higher classes can be regarded as the logical ' *genus* ' of the class beneath, and is so, not merely because it includes a larger number of individuals, but because it expresses some real character held in common by the *species* or classes beneath, of which it is the *genus*. If we may suppose a botanist who has never before come across the name *Vicia faba*, the first time he hears it, he will from its form know two things about the specimen it denotes, (1) that it partakes of the common fund of ' *Vicia*-ness ', and (2) that it differs in some feature or features from all the other *Vicia's* he knows.

The Eulerian Diagrams

Various systems of diagrams have been invented from time to time to help the student to understand and remember the logical relations between subject and predicate in the various types of proposition. If the student finds them a help, well and good ; but he may find them of little assistance, and an additional burden, especially if he is not of a mathematical turn of mind—in which case he should pass them by ; they are not of the essence of Logic. Diagrams in any case must be received with reserve ; they have one great drawback for the average man ; they limit attention to the mathematical aspects of propositions. Diagrams, being spatial representations, can only represent the extension and denotation of terms, their classes and the individuals in the classes ; they fail to represent the deeper meaning of terms, their intension and connotation.

The most influential system is that of the Swiss mathematician, Euler (1707–83).[1] His system makes one circle (S) stand for the subject and another circle (P) stand for the predicate. The two circles are then paired off in five different ways, according as the two circles cut one another, or include one another (two cases), or exclude one another, or coincide. There are thus five diagrams, which between them cover all the ways in which the subject of a proposition can be related to its predicate by way of extension. The diagrams can be used to illustrate the distribution of the predicate, the opposition and conversion of propositions, and other forms of immediate inference. The system can be applied to the rules of syllogism. The order of the diagrams and the number assigned to each differ in different textbooks. Keynes adopts the following order and numeration:

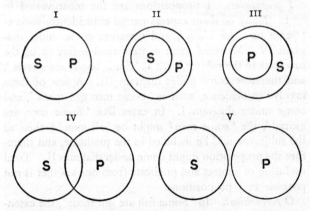

[1] Also to be mentioned are the systems of the German logician, Lambert (1728–77), and of the Cambridge logician, J. Venn (1834–1923). These systems together with Euler's are explained in *Formal Logic*, by J. N. Keynes, Part II, ch. IV.

There is no exact correspondence between the five diagrams and the four types of propositions, A, E, I, and O. All E propositions fall under one diagram, viz. No. V, and some O propositions fall under No. V. A, I, and O propositions all require more diagrams than one.

A propositions. In a few A propositions, such as ' All men can speak ', subject and predicate are virtually co-extensive, and they are therefore represented by diagram I. In the great majority of A propositions, such as ' All men are mortal ', or ' All philosophers speculate ', the predicate is wider than the subject, and they are therefore represented by diagram II.

E propositions. In all E propositions no S is P, and no P is S ; i.e. S and P lie completely outside one another in respect of their extension and denotation. Therefore all E propositions are represented by diagram V.

I propositions. I propositions are the most varied in type. Many of them express partial coincidence, such as ' Some men are black ', and therefore come under diagram IV. Many of them express total inclusion of the predicate in the subject, such as ' Some books are novels ', and therefore come under diagram III. A few of them involve coincidence, such as ' Some men can speak ', and come under diagram I. In cases like ' Some men are mortal ', the ' some men ' might be ' all men ' ; then all the subject would be included in the predicate, and therefore the proposition might come under diagram II. Total exclusion of subject and predicate from one another is not possible in I propositions.

O propositions. In ' Some fish are not trout ', the extension and denotation of *trout* lie entirely within that of *fish* and therefore it and other O propositions, like it, come under diagram III. In ' Some men are not brown ',

subject and predicate coincide partially, and such propositions come under diagram IV.   In ' Some sunny days are
not good for angling' the subject of course is undistributed.   In anticyclone weather all sunny days put fish
down and are bad for angling.   If under such conditions
' Some sunny days ' proves to mean ' All sunny days ',
the O proposition would prove to be E, and subject and
predicate would fall completely outside one another, and
would come under diagram V.   The foregoing analysis
is summarized in the following table.

TYPES OF PROPOSITIONS AND THE EULERIAN DIAGRAMS

A propositions .	.	I or II, but not III or IV or V
E „	.	V, but not I or II or III or IV
I „	.	I or II or III or IV, but not V
O „	.	III or IV or V, but not I or II

Questions and Exercises on Chapter VII

1. What did the word ' category ' mean to the Greeks?
Aristotle gave it a technical sense.

2. List Aristotle's Categories, illustrating each.   Which was
the leading category for him?   Why?   Is the list of practical
value today?

3. How do Predicables differ from Categories?

4. Sketch the history of the doctrine of the Predicables.

5. What is a *Property* in logic?   Specify a property of man.
Is it correct to speak of an ' essential property '?

6. What is the origin of the word ' differentiate '?

7. How are *genus* and *species* related?   Can a *genus* be also a
species ?

8. Show from the history of botany how the need for
classification arises.   And how systems of classification are
modified and developed.

9. Diagrams in logic have advantages and disadvantages.
Explain Euler's system.

CHAPTER VIII

SYLLOGISTIC ARGUMENTS. FALLACIES

Enthymeme[1]

An Enthymeme is a syllogism with one premiss or the conclusion suppressed. It is in fact an abbreviated syllogism, such as those that occur in actual discourse or in writing. To express all three propositions would be pedantry in most contexts, and bad policy. The art of convincing often lies in hiding the fact that you are trying to convince. Hearers or readers, confronted with the paraphernalia of syllogistic argument, are on their guard, and the combative instinct is aroused. Partly for policy, and partly from laziness, if we want to ' get a syllogism across', as a rule we utter no more of it than is necessary, and we leave the rest to the imagination. Any two of the three constituent propositions are usually enough to suggest the third.

A premiss, major or minor, is left unsaid because, as a rule, it says itself. The suppression of the conclusion is not so common. When done, it is done for effect, and it can be a most effective device. A suppressed conclusion is like a sword suspended by a hair, not falling, but ever ready to fall. Innuendos are often conveyed in this way, and pointed thrusts which words would blunt. Examples:

Major premiss suppressed. Afforestation schemes remove land from cultivation, and are therefore of little benefit to the neighbourhood. The suppressed major is: All schemes that remove land from cultivation are of little benefit to the neighbourhood.

---

[1] Aristotle used the term in quite a different sense. He says " an enthymeme is a syllogism starting from probabilities or signs ". *Analytica Priora*, II, 27, 70a.

Minor premiss suppressed. Long-term investments, essential to the national economy, ultimately benefit every part of the country. Therefore afforestation schemes ultimately benefit every part of the country. The implied minor is : Afforestation schemes are long-term investments, essential to the national economy.

Conclusion suppressed. Cain hates his brother, and he that hates his brother is a murderer. The conclusion ' Cain is a murderer ' is suppressed.

Polysyllogisms.   Sorites[1]

Several syllogisms, joined together like links in a chain, the conclusion of one forming a premiss for another, make a Polysyllogism. St. Paul's argument in Romans viii 29-30 is in the nature of a polysyllogism, " For whom he did foreknow, he also did predestinate . . . Moreover whom he did predestinate, them he also called ; and whom he called, them he also justified ; and whom he justified, them he also glorified."

The most interesting type of polysyllogism is the Sorites ; the word comes from the Greek σωρός, a heap. The Sorites is a heaped argument ; it is defined as *A polysyllogism in the first figure, with the intermediate conclusions suppressed, and supplied mentally as minor premisses with the following major premiss.* It has the form :

Sorites	Suppressed Conclusions
A is B	
B is C	∴ A is C
C is D	∴ A is D
D is E	∴ A is E
E is F	
∴ A is F	

[1] Three syllables ; pronounced Saw-ri-tees.

The minor premiss is written first, then its major premiss; each suppressed conclusion becomes in turn minor premiss to the subsequent major premiss. The predicate of each premiss is subject of the next, and the subject of the first premiss, and the predicate of the last premiss are, respectively, subject and predicate of the final conclusion. The first and second premisses are minor and major, respectively, of the first syllogism; its conclusion (suppressed) and the third premiss are minor and major, respectively, of the second syllogism; and so on, till the conclusion of the Sorites is reached.

The Sorites has two rules:

> *The first premiss alone can be particular.*
> *The last premiss alone can be negative.*

To prove these rules break the Sorites up into its component syllogisms. The first premiss is minor of the first syllogism, and each suppressed conclusion acts in turn as minor of the next following syllogism. If the first premiss is particular, the intermediate and final conclusions will be particular; but if any premiss, other than the first, were particular, there would of necessity be an undistributed middle in the syllogism that contained it; for each expressed premiss after the first acts as major, having as subject the middle term, which is required to be distributed there, since it is undistributed in the corresponding minor, which is affirmative and has the middle term as predicate. Therefore the first premiss alone can be particular.

The last premiss can be negative, and if it is negative, the conclusion of the whole Sorites is negative. No other premiss can be negative; for if it were, there would be an Illicit Process of the major term in the syllogism, next following. All the intermediate conclusions, as we have seen, serve as minor, each in the syllogism, next following; they must therefore be affirmative; for a negative minor would require the major to be affirmative and its predicate, the major term, to be undistributed, and the conclusion to be negative and its predicate, the major term, to be distributed. Therefore the last premiss alone can be negative.

In their more familiar form and order (1) The minor premiss must be affirmative, and (2) The major premiss must be universal, these rules echo the Special Rules of the first figure, the Sorites being composed of first figure syllogisms.[1]

Hypothetical and Disjunctive Syllogisms

These reasonings have much in common with syllogisms in their inward movement, though unlike in outward form. They have no middle term; the rules of syllogism do not only apply to them, and Aristotle does not call them syllogisms. The title *syllogism* can, however, be justified on broad grounds. Though the reasoning is complex, it is of the syllogistic order. Some Categorical syllogisms can be set out as hypothetical reasoning, and some hypothetical arguments transpose easily into syllogistic form. 'If he sows little, he reaps little' is first cousin to 'All who sow little reap little', and to 'Niggard sowers are niggard reapers'. The Categorical syllogism,

> All who teach themselves logic are well taught.
> He teaches himself logic.
> ∴ He is well taught.

[1] Sorites in other figures are theoretically possible; but they do not occur normally.

differs little from the Hypothetical,

> If he teaches himself logic, he is well taught.
> He teaches himself logic.
> ∴ He is well taught.

The word *If* has subtle shades of meaning.[1] Sometimes the conditional element is strong, and then the transposition of the argument to the Categorical form is not so natural. Sometimes *If* means little more than *Whenever*, and then the transposition is natural and easy. Compare

> *If* he is sick, he sends for the doctor.

with

> *If* ' if's ' and ' an's ' were pots and pans,
> There'ld be no work for the tinkers' hands.

Hypothetical Syllogisms[2]

A Hypothetical syllogism with both premisses and the conclusion hypothetical is called *Pure*. It is a valid mode of argument, but it is not in common use; for its constituent propositions (as the politician said at the news conference) are too ' iffy '. Example:

> If the play is good, the audience will not eat chocolates.
> If the actors know their parts, the play is good.
> ∴ If the actors know their parts, the audience will not eat chocolates.

---

[1] See above. p. 57.
[2] Here the reader should refresh his memory about the Hypothetical proposition, which was explained above (p. 56). Those who wish a fuller discussion of the *Pure* Hypothetical Syllogism (together with a distinction between Conditional and Hypothetical propositions) should see J. N. Keynes, *Formal Logic*, 4th ed., Pt. II, ch. ix, and Pt. III, ch. v.

In the normal Hypothetical syllogism which is in frequent use, one premiss, usually called the major, is a hypothetical proposition, and the other premiss, usually called the minor, and the conclusion are categorical propositions. In a valid Hypothetical syllogism the categorical minor affirms the antecedent of the major, or denies its consequent, not *vice versa*; while the conclusion affirms the consequent or denies the antecedent, not *vice versa*. If the conclusion affirms the consequent, the syllogism is constructive, and its mood is known as *Modus Ponens*, because it lays down (*ponere*) a truth. If it denies the antecedent, the syllogism is destructive, and its mood is known as *Modus Tollens* because it removes (*tollere*) an error. Examples:

MODUS PONENS

If A is B, it is C.	If A is B, X is Y.
A is B.	A is B.
∴ It is C.	∴ X is Y.

If man has free-will, he is responsible for his actions.
Man has free-will.
∴ He is responsible for his actions.

If it is freezing, we shall have skating.
It is freezing.
∴ We shall have skating.

N.B. The quality of the constituent clauses of the Hypothetical major has nothing to say to the mood of the syllogism. Both the following syllogisms are in *Modus Ponens*, though they contain negative clauses; they both posit, i.e. establish, something, even though what is established is a negative proposition.

If the rain does not fall, the salmon will not run.
The rain does not fall.
∴ The salmon will not run.

If the cat's at home, the mice will not play.
The cat's at home.
∴ The mice will not play.

MODUS TOLLENS

If A is B, it is C.	If A is B, X is Y.
A is not C.	X is not Y.
∴ It is not B.	∴ A is not B.

If he gives the soft answer, he turns away wrath.
He does not turn away wrath.
∴ He does not give the soft answer.

If the cricket XI wins the cup, the school gets a half-holiday.
The school does not get a half-holiday.
∴ The cricket XI does not win the cup.

People can easily go wrong in hypothetical reasoning. They mistake good arguments for bad, and bad arguments for good. It is a case where natural logic is not enough. Training and training-rules are required. The rules for distinguishing good and bad are clear and definite, and they spring from the nature of hypothesis and supposing; but students often find them confusing, and they would be well advised to make a special effort at the outset to get them clear in the mind. I make the following suggestions: (1) Memorize the four rules listed below (*a*, *α*, *b*, *β*). (2) Apply them to instances of your own choosing. In other words, make up hypothetical syllogisms; bring them under the rules, and decide for yourself whether they are valid, or not. (3) Avoid negative clauses in the major at first. There is nothing wrong with them, but they are confusing. (4) There is only one valid argument in each of the two moods, but corresponding to each of the two valid arguments there is a plausible invalid argument (a 'trap for the unwary', as we might say). It is well therefore to formulate *four* Rules in all, two Rules of Inference, two Rules of non-Inference, two to let in the good arguments, and two to keep out the bad. They are:

(*a*) From the truth of the antecedent we can infer the truth of the consequent; but (α) From the truth of the consequent we cannot infer the truth of the antecedent.

(*b*) From the falsity of the consequent we can infer the falsity of the antecedent; but (β) From the falsity of the antecedent we cannot infer the falsity of the consequent.

Examples (using the same terms):

Valid arguments	*Invalid arguments*
(*a*) If it is freezing, we shall have skating. It is freezing. ∴ We shall have skating.	(α) If it is freezing, we shall have skating. We shall have skating. ∴ It is freezing. (No. That is a fallacy; our skating will be roller-skating.)
(*b*) If it is freezing, we shall have skating. We shall not have skating. ∴ It is not freezing.	(β) If it is freezing, we shall have skating. It is not freezing. ∴ We shall not have skating. (Yes. We shall; roller-skating.)

The Disjunctive Syllogism

Here the student should refer back to pp. 58 ff., and refresh his memory on the constitution and purpose of the Disjunctive Proposition, paying special attention to the distinction between the two types of disjunction, Exclusive and Non-exclusive.

A Disjunctive Syllogism is one which has a Disjunctive

Proposition as major premiss, and as minor premiss a Cate-
gorical Proposition, affirming or denying one of the alternatives
in the major premiss, and a conclusion denying or affirming
the other alternative. If the conclusion *denies*, the mood
is *Ponendo Tollens*, so-called because by establishing (*ponendo*)
the minor premiss, it destroys (*tollens*) the other alternative.
If the conclusion *affirms*, the mood is *Tollendo Ponens*, so-
called because by destroying (*tollendo*) the minor premiss,
the syllogism establishes (*ponens*) the other alternative.
Examples :

MODUS PONENDO TOLLENS

A is either B or C.　　　　He is either a fool or a knave.
A is B.　　　　　　　　　He is a fool.
∴ A is not C.　　　　　　∴ He is not a knave.

Either A is B or C is D.　Either the train left early, or he
　　　　　　　　　　　　　reached the station late.
A is B.　　　　　　　　　The train left early.
∴ C is not D.　　　　　　∴ He did not reach the station late.

Either A or B is C.　　　　Either Oxford or Cambridge won
　　　　　　　　　　　　　the boat race.
A is C.　　　　　　　　　Oxford won.
∴ B is not C.　　　　　　∴ Cambridge did not win.

The student is probably not altogether satisfied with
these arguments. They look plausible ; some are convincing, but some are not. The fact is that there has long
been a doubt about this mood, Ponendo Tollens. We
cannot say it is valid in all cases ; nor can we say it is
invalid in all cases. It all depends whether the alternatives
stated in the major are mutually exclusive ; if they are,
the argument is valid ; if not, not. *There is no way of*

knowing from the form alone, whether the alternatives are mutually exclusive. Some urge that they ought to be mutually exclusive, if the form were properly used; but that is a matter of opinion. It is often a convenience to use the disjunctive form in both ways, just as it is a convenience to use an envelope both for the address and the correspondence. We must take each case on its merits, must try and decide from the contents whether the alternatives are mutually exclusive, and must allow for the doubtful case.

Of the six examples given above the three in symbols are unrevealing. Not knowing what the letters stand for, we have no information on the crucial point, and do not know whether the alternatives are mutually exclusive, or not, and we cannot say whether they represent valid arguments, or not.

Of the three concrete examples, the first is arguable. Arguing from the general nature of man, we should say that he might be both fool and knave, in which case the conclusion would be invalid. But if we knew the man in question and the full facts of the case, we might well mean by the major premiss that the man has committed either a foolish act or a knavish act, and not both—in which case the conclusion would be valid.

The second concrete example is *on the evidence* invalid. There is nothing stated, and there is nothing in the nature of things to make the alternatives mutually exclusive. It is quite possible that the station clock was fast and so the train left early, *and* that the man overslept and so reached the station late. If we know, however, that the man was a paragon of punctuality and that his alarm-clock and the station clock were electrically synchronized, this possibility would be reduced almost to *zero*; the two alternatives

F

would become mutually exclusive to all intents and purposes, and therefore the conclusion would be valid.

The last example is clearly valid. Cambridge could not *win*, if Oxford *won*. We are sure of it from the word *won* and the nature of a race, not from the 'either . . . or' and the form of a disjunction. Races can be drawn or abandoned, or in other ways fail to yield a result; but if one competitor won (as is stated in this instance), it stands to reason that the other did not win. Those who say that 'won' in the minor might mean only 'were not beaten' are taking a liberty with language which would make nonsense of the major. The alternatives from the nature of the race and the ordinary use of words are mutually exclusive.

From these examples it becomes clear that men use the disjunctive form of reasoning, not in the abstract, but in relation to their own knowledge and that of those with whom they are conversing. They are quite right to do so, and we logicians have no right to complain. Logic would be a little simpler if these ambiguities did not exist; but Logic was made for man, not man for Logic. The attempt has been made to separate 'the pure disjunctive form' from 'the mixed alternative'; but language would lose by the separation; it is better to keep the disjunctive form, as men habitually use it, with its inherent and (often) valuable ambiguity, explaining its uses and giving warning of its abuses, as logicians for centuries have done.

MODUS TOLLENDO PONENS

This is the more useful of the two moods; for it establishes affirmations, and there is no doubt about its validity; while the other mood, *Ponendo Tollens*, establishes denials, and their validity, as we have seen, can in particular cases be challenged.   Examples :

A is either B or C.	It is either a bush or a bear.
A is not B.	It is not a bush.
∴ A is C.	∴ It is a bear.

Either A is B, or C is D.	Either the cartridge was old, or I shot wide.
A is not B.	The cartridge was not old.
∴ C is D.	∴ I shot wide.

Either A or B is C.	Either physic or faith cured the fever.
A is not C.	Physic did not cure the fever.
∴ B is C.	∴ Faith did.

These are all valid inferences ; the student should compare them with the examples of the other mood, noting the points of difference. In *Tollendo Ponens* the minor *denies* one of the alternatives, and the conclusion *affirms* the other ; in *Ponendo Tollens* the minor *affirms* one of the alternatives, and the conclusion *denies* the other. Here lies the strength of *Ponens* and the weakness of *Tollens*. The nature of disjunction is such that by denying one alternative, we establish the other, but by establishing one alternative we do not necessarily deny the other.

To simplify the exposition of this difficult form I have confined myself to disjunctions with only two members. Many disjunctions have three or more members, but they involve no new principle. In *Tollendo Ponens* we can argue validly from the denial of all but one, to the affirmation of that one, or from the denial of all but two to the affirmation of those two as alternatives. From ' The animal is either lost or stolen or strayed ', if it was not lost or stolen, we can infer that it strayed ; and if it was not stolen, we can infer that it was lost or that it strayed. In the case of *Ponendo Tollens* with three or more members the doubt as to its validity remains, as outlined above, in particular cases.

N.B. In discussing this subtle form the student must always bear in mind the distinction between truth and validity. As logicians we are only concerned with whether the conclusion follows from the given premisses. In framing such premisses, as distinct from arguing from them, we must consider whether the stated alternatives are exhaustive, and whether mixtures and combinations of alternatives are possible.

The Dilemma

By derivation a Dilemma is a double-grip argument, a two-pronged fork. In ordinary speech the word has lost much of its original force, and now means little more than a quandary or an unpleasant alternative. To the logician it has long been a delicate and intriguing piece of mental machinery, and from ancient days it has been the darling child of the rhetoricians. From the frequent use made of it in controversy, it derives its unpleasant associations.

The Dilemma combines hypothetical and disjunctive reasoning. A good working definition is that of Whately,[1] *A syllogism which has a conditional major premiss, with more than one antecedent, and a disjunctive minor premiss.* It fails to cover, however, some cases of the Simple Destructive Dilemma. Joseph[2] offers the rather wide definition,

---

[1] Whately, R. (1787–1863), Archbishop of Dublin, author of *Logic* 1826, and other works.
[2] *op. cit.*, p. 358.

A hypothetical argument offering alternatives and proving something against an opponent in either case. If the Dilemma affirms the antecedent (antecedents) of the major, it is called Constructive ; if it denies the consequent (consequents), it is called Destructive. If the conclusion is the same whichever alternative is accepted, it is called Simple ; if different, it is called Complex. Examples :

SIMPLE CONSTRUCTIVE

If either A is B or C is D, E is F.
But either A is B or C is D.
∴ E is F.

If either he travels by train or flies, he will be in time for the
    meeting.
But either he travels by train or flies.
∴ He will be in time for the meeting.

COMPLEX CONSTRUCTIVE

If A is B, E is F, and if C is D, G is H.
But either A is B or C is D.
∴ Either E is F or G is H.

If I go by bus, I shall have to wait till the office opens, and if
    I walk, I shall be late.
But either I go by bus, or I walk.
∴ Either I shall have to wait till the office opens, or I shall be
    late.

SIMPLE DESTRUCTIVE

If A is B, C is D and E is F.
But either C is not D or E is not F.
∴ A is not B.

If A is B, either C is D or E is F.
But neither is C D, nor is E F.
∴ A is not B.

If bodies can move, they must move either where they are or
 where they are not.
Bodies cannot move either where they are or where they are not.
∴ Bodies cannot move.[1]

COMPLEX DESTRUCTIVE

If A is B, E is F, and if C is D, G is H.
But either E is not F, or G is not H.
∴ Either A is not B, or C is not D.

If a man has unfettered freedom of choice, he is responsible
 for all his actions, and if he has a completely moral nature,
 he must be fully aware of it.
But either a man is not responsible for all his actions, or he is
 not fully aware of his moral nature.
∴ Either he has not unfettered freedom of choice, or he has
 not a completely moral nature.

The ancients pictured the alternatives as *horns*, because
if you escaped one, you were liable to be impaled on the
other. Hence the phrase 'the horns of a dilemma'.
Keeping up the metaphor they listed three ways of meeting
an attack by dilemma, to escape between the horns, to
take it by the horns, and to rebut it. *To escape between the
horns* is to find another alternative. A body might move
from where it is to where it is not. That suggestion offers
a disputant a verbal escape, at least, between the horns of
Zeno's paradox. To 'take a dilemma by the horns' is
to accept one or both of the alternatives, but to deny the
alleged consequence. A man might accept unfettered
freedom of choice, but might deny that it involved responsi-
bility for all his actions. Or he might accept a completely
moral nature, while denying the necessity of full conscious-
ness of it. Rebuttal consists in producing another dilemma

[1] One of Zeno's paradoxes of motion; it is used by Joseph, *op. cit.*
p. 359, where see his discussion of the definition of *dilemma*.

with a conclusion which contradicts, or appears to contradict, the original conclusion. The Greeks invented several clever rebuttals. The most famous, known as *Litigiosus*, ran as follows :

Protagoras agreed to teach Euathlus the art of rhetoric. Half of the fee was to be paid at the end of the course of instruction, and the other half when Euathlus won his first case at law. The instruction was given, and the first moiety was paid. Euathlus did nothing further in the matter. He brought no action in the Courts, and pleaded no case. In need of money Protagoras took the initiative and sued Euathlus for the balance of his fee. Protagoras put his case to the Court in the form of this dilemma—If Euathlus wins the case, he must pay me by the terms of our agreement. If he loses, he must pay me by order of the Court. He must either win the case or lose it. Therefore in either event he must pay me. Euathlus rebutted, as follows—If I win the case, I do not pay by order of the Court, and if I lose the case, I do not pay under the terms of our agreement. But I must either win the case or lose it. Therefore in either event I do not pay.

Analogy

A brief discussion of Analogy may serve to link deductive Logic to inductive ; for analogy is an inference from a resemblance between particular things, events, or occasions to a further resemblance. Peisistratus, a political leader at Athens, asked for a bodyguard, and by means of it made himself tyrant. On this analogy, said Aristotle, it might have been inferred that when Dionysius of Syracuse asked for a bodyguard, he was aiming at supreme power.

Analogy always contains a pinch of uncertainty, and is therefore distinct from logical inference. Good democrats have been known to ask for a bodyguard. The analogy may hold, or it may not. Yet in spite of the uncertainty analogy and logical inference have much in common; they both build on the *genus*, the kind, the repeated instance. " Probability is the very guide of life ",[1] wrote Bishop Butler, and analogy is probability, systematically used, consciously directed, and woven into experience. I am driving a car in traffic; an urchin darts across my driving-field, nimbly threads his risky way, and reaches the safety of the pavement. Though he is safe, instinctively I slow down; for where there is one urchin, there is probably another. Arguing on analogy I expect him, too, to dart across; for he, too, argues on analogy unconsciously, and seeing his chum make the crossing safely expects a similar success.[2]

Likeness and repetition—these are the foundations of analogy. Where they are not, there is no analogy; where they are found, there is a basis, however slight, for analogical inference. We expect the sun to rise tomorrow, because we think of tomorrow on the analogy of yesterday and today. We notice similarities in the changing altitudes of the sun, in the waxing and waning of the light, and in our own sensations of freshness and fatigue; when we lie down to rest, on analogy we expect to wake up next morning refreshed, and to find the sun arising or arisen. Analogy attends and uses belief in the uniformity of nature and in natural law. Because objects or the relations

---

[1] J. Butler (1692–1752), *The Analogy of Religion*, Introduction, 1736.
[2] The probability which comes close to Analogy and in practice guides a large part of human life must be distinguished from the Probability which is confined to the numerical and calculable aspects of events and is treated in the mathematical Theory of Probability.

between objects are alike in some points we conclude by analogy that they are alike in other points also, and therefore analogy enters into the inferential processes of induction (see below, pp. 172 ff.).

Conscious analogy was originally based only on identical relations, or very similar relations. It involved four terms, and was seen at its best in mathematics. Such analogy is in fact proportion; a is to b, as c is to d. If we know that the size of London is to that of Dublin as 10 to 1, and know the area of either city, we know the area of the other. Given the population of London we could form some idea of that of Dublin; but if we went on to argue that London must have ten times as many cathedrals and churches and art galleries as Dublin we should be pushing analogy too far.

Resemblances other than those of size, distance, and number are less reliable as a basis for analogy. A minister or parish priest is like a shepherd in his duties to his flock, and the ' flock ' are like sheep in respect of their spiritual needs; outside that area the analogy soon breaks down.

Analogy is simpler when there are just two terms and their resemblances. The man is like his portrait; harm his portrait, says black magic, and you harm the man. The looser analogies of quality are often more penetrating than the strict analogies of quantity. An analogy of quality, such as that implicit in the phrase ' mother-earth ' or ' fatherland ', may touch the heart of things, while a relation of quantity may only scratch the surface. In estimating the value of an analogy we must have regard to its character and relevance and real connection with the inferred resemblance. Apparent strength can be deceptive, and quite faint analogies have led at times to great discoveries. In using analogies caution is necessary.

A's meat is B's poison. The medicine that cured Lucy may not cure a neighbour's child. J. S. Mill who uses this example happily compares analogy to a sign-post, which may point the direction, but does not get you there.[1] 'False Analogy' is a recognized fallacy.

Fallacies

Men err, and most men err in similar ways. The stock errors in logic to which the human mind is prone have long been named and listed. They are known as Fallacies, i.e. Deceptive Arguments. To be made aware of them, to know their names and just why they are fallacies, is part of the discipline of logic. They are not the only fallacies; but they are the chief ones. Every rule in logic can be broken, and from that angle there are just as many fallacies as there are rules.

In syllogistic reasoning the three main Fallacies are:

(1) *Undistributed Middle.* Example:

All followers of Izaak Walton love virtue and angling.

Jones loves virtue and angling.

∴ He is a follower of Izaak Walton.

The middle term 'love virtue and angling' is undistributed in both premisses; therefore the conclusion does not follow from the premisses, and the syllogism is fallacious.

People who judge by general impression and not by rule fall readily into this fallacy. In the above instance Jones clearly is a follower of Izaak Walton in the ordinary meaning of that term. None the less that proposition cannot be inferred from the given premisses, and for all

[1] J. S. Mill, *op. cit.*, Bk. III, c. xx, 3; cf. Bk. II, iii, 3.

we (as logicians) know to the contrary, there may be a 'splinter' group of virtuous anglers who owe no allegiance to the *Compleat Angler* and its author.

(2) *Illicit Process.* This fallacy consists in taking universally in the conclusion a term given particularly in its premiss; that is, in arguing from a term given undistributed to the same term distributed. Illicit Process may be of the major, or of the minor. Examples:

Of the major	Of the minor
Some clever men are eccentric.	All rooks are gregarious.
Smith is not eccentric.	Some crows are not gregarious.
∴ He is not a clever man.	∴ No crows are rooks.

(3) *Two Middle Terms.* Examples:

Chalk is different from cheese.	Nothing is better than wisdom.
Cheese is different from butter.	A crust is better than nothing.
∴ Butter is different from chalk.	∴ A crust is better than wisdom.

They are only pseudo-syllogisms, of course, and are not to be taken seriously; but in the first case, *cheese* and *different from cheese* look like middle terms, and in the second case *nothing* and *better than nothing* might convey a similar impression. In all such cases set out the supposed syllogism 'in logical form', and the fallacy would be exposed at once. Resignation as a Christian virtue, and Resignation as retirement from office, are different things, and premisses which used the one word in the two senses would be fallacious. The fallacy would be that of *Ambiguous Middle Term* which is a variety of *Two Middle Terms*, and is also known as the Fallacy of *Four Terms*, in Latin, *Quaternio Terminorum*.

Aristotle's Lists of Fallacies[1]

Aristotle did not include among the Fallacies plain breaches of the rules of inference, such as the foregoing. He confined his lists to linguistic forms and faults in thinking that habitually lead men astray in argument. He distinguished fallacies in speech (*in dictione*) from other fallacies (*extra dictionem*), and he made two corresponding lists, with six fallacies in the former list, and seven in the latter. His treatment is open to criticism; his types overlap, and his fallacies *extra dictionem* are in part concerned with the right use of words. But still his work on the fallacies was invaluable in its day; it was a pioneer and penetrating achievement, rendered necessary by the sophistry of his day, and the methods of disputation to which the sophists[2] gave currency. It is of value still, and is enshrined in the outlook and the language of European culture.

Fallacies in Dictione

(1) Equivocation. To equivocate is to make illegitimate use of ambiguous words. The practice is misleading, and may often burke the issue. The term *old*, for instance, may mean the old in years, or the men of old time. Hence the following syllogism ' equivocates ' and is fallacious :

The old are more likely to be right in their judgment than the young.

[1] The full Lists are given for completeness' sake. The beginner should not attempt to memorize them, but should read them sympathetically for their historic interest, remembering that even those fallacies that look to us trivial have become *so* largely as a result of Aristotle's work.

[2] The Sophists were the pioneers of higher education in ancient Greece. Their movement fell into disrepute, because their methods and principles, broadly speaking, subordinated truth to expediency.

The men who wrote a thousand years ago are old writers.
∴ They are more likely to be right in their judgment
than those of our own day.[1]

Unintentional equivocation almost inevitably creeps into
long arguments on religion, philosophy, ethics, politics,
etc. Words like *right* and *good*, *happiness* and *pleasure*,
church and *state*, *government* and *people*, are apt to take their
colour from their context, as the chameleon is said to do,
and it is hard to pin them down to one precise, invariable
meaning. One must try one's best to be consistent.

(2) Amphiboly. Amphiboly is ambiguity in phrasing,
and is not quite the same as Equivocation, though often
the line between them is very fine. The ancient oracles
made frequent use of both ambiguities. In a famous
amphiboly King Croesus was informed that if he attacked
the Persians, he would destroy a great empire. Whether
the 'great empire' was his own or that of the Persians,
the oracle did not disclose.

(3) Composition. The fallacy of Composition is the
illegitimate compounding of words or objects of thought,
as in 'Five and two are odd and even; therefore seven
is odd and even'. This fallacy readily occurs when *all*
(collective) is understood as *all* (distributive). All the
XI made 10 runs; therefore the whole side made 110 runs;
or was their total just 10 runs? The humorous suggestion
of the epitaph on Robert Boyle, 'He was father of
Chemistry and brother of the Earl of Cork' depends on
the mental Composition of the notions of spiritual and
physical relationship; but of course the epitaph as such
is not fallacious.

(4) Division. The fallacy of Division is the converse

[1] From T. K. Abbott, *Elements of Logic*, p. 86.

of the preceding, and it is often hard to keep the two apart. The stock instance which traces to Aristotle is 'Three and two are odd and even; therefore three and two are odd and three and two are even.' Similarly it might be argued that if my neighbour and I share a party wall, we each own half a party wall; or that if the clergy and congregation contributed £100 to the Organ Fund, the clergy contributed £100 and the congregation another £100; and one could sub-divide both groups.

(5) Accent. Tone accent and stress and italics can completely alter the meaning of words, and render an argument fallacious. All invalids take tonic, and all fallacies are invalid; but of course those facts provide no basis for inference.

(6) Figure of Speech. Originally a 'Figure of speech' meant a verbal inflexion which was ambiguous and gave rise to a fallacy if an argument was based on it. A Frenchman with a smattering of English was thanked by his English friend for his 'invaluable services'. Monsieur took offence; knowing that *inaudible* and *inaccurate* were the opposites, respectively, of *audible* and *accurate*, he argued from the Figure of Speech—the prefix ' in-'— that *invaluable* was the opposite of *valuable*. Today the phrase covers 'Figures of Syntax'. In ' Mr Weller took his hat and his leave ' and ' She came home in a sedan chair and floods of tears ' the figurative and the literal are combined. Phrases like ' took his leave ' and ' in floods of tears ' are figures of speech, which with all tropes and metaphors are to be avoided in serious argument.

Fallacies Extra Dictionem

(1) Accident. According to Aristotle the fallacy arises " whenever any attribute is claimed to belong in a like

manner to a thing and to its accident ".[1] The sophists argued that the dog was a father and was yours; therefore he was your father. Aristotle called this trick of speech a fallacy of Accident. The argument presumes that the animal is yours as a father, as he is yours as a dog. Today *Accident* and *Secundum Quid* are hardly distinguishable.

(2) *Secundum Quid.* In full, *A Dicto simpliciter ad Dictum secundum quid*—which means, From something said simply to something said *according to something*, i.e. with a qualification. Joseph[2] describes *Secundum Quid* as " one of the subtlest and commonest sources of error. It consists in using a principle or proposition without regard to the circumstances which modify its applicability in the case or kind of case before us." This broad way of expressing the fallacy makes it unnecessary to distinguish between *A Dicto simpliciter ad Dictum secundum quid*, and, *A Dicto secundum quid ad Dictum simpliciter*. In both cases the qualification is ignored whether at the head or the tail of the argument. ' Thou shalt not kill ' is a *Dictum simpliciter*. ' Thou shalt do no murder' is the same *Dictum, secundum quid*. For *murder* is not simply *killing*, but *taking human life wrongfully*. Not all killing is murder. Theologians, moralists, and lawyers have to consider the distinction with the greatest care, and advise the State accordingly. The logician has to call attention to the fallacy of arguing from a qualified statement to an unqualified, or *vice versa*. In the argument,[3]

> Opium is a poison.
> Physicians give their patients opium.
> ∴ They give their patients poison.

---

[1] *De Sophisticis Elenchis*, V, 166b.   [2] *op. cit.*, p. 589.
[3] From T. K. Abbott, *op. cit.*, p. 88.

the fallacy is latent, rather than explicit. All three propositions are statements of fact, until the third is understood in a bad sense; and then the fallacy becomes explicit; the qualification 'for remedial purposes', implied in the second and third propositions, has been ignored.

(3) *Ignoratio Elenchi*. It is a legal phrase; for the *elenchus* in Greek law was the refutation of the charge; and *ignoratio elenchi* means ignorance of, or ignoring, the charge to be refuted. The counsel who does not 'know his brief' or who ignores it, cannot refute the charge, and is reduced to spending time and eloquence in proving what no one denies, in proving the irrelevant, or in 'abusing the plaintiff's attorney'. Similarly the disputant who does not, or will not, understand the matter in dispute, and who avoids or confuses the issue, or proves what is beside the point, or passes off some irrelevance for proof, is guilty of *ignoratio elenchi*.

An *Argumentum ad hominem* is not necessarily a fallacy; but if it is, it comes under this head; for the fallacious arguer would fail to grasp the real issue, as it presents itself to those with whom he is arguing.

An *Argumentum ad hominem* is an argument addressed to a man. This may mean one of two things. (*a*) Instead of attacking the statement we attack the man who makes it. When politicians, or others, instead of refuting a line of policy, attack the character or motives of its advocate, they are arguing *ad hominem*, instead of *ad rem*. (*b*) More often an argument is called *ad hominem* (or, *ad homines*), when its premisses are admitted by some of those who hear it, but not by all. It is a sectional argument, valid for those who accept the premisses, but not for the others. Examples :

> No just wars are *per se* immoral.
> Defensive wars are just wars.
> ∴ Defensive wars are not *per se* immoral.

Actions that involve taking human life are unconditionally wrong.
Defensive wars are actions that involve taking human life.
∴ Defensive wars are unconditionally wrong.

Both these arguments are *ad homines*; for their major premisses would be accepted by one group of thinkers, and rejected by another group; and those who accept the premisses must accept the conclusions. There is nothing illogical or fallacious so far; there is nothing illogical or fallacious in an argument *ad homines* as such. It only becomes a fallacy when he who accepts a conclusion on behalf of those who endorse its premisses, goes on to use it *as if it had been universally accepted*.

(4) *Petitio Principii*. The name means ' Asking for the Principle '; in English it is called ' Begging the Question '. The Principle or Question is the conclusion before it is proved. To ' beg ' it is to ask for it to be granted in advance. We beg the question, when we assume the conclusion to be true, and use it as a premiss in a different form of words, and from it draw the desired conclusion. In this way of proceeding, there is no advance. The conclusion is drawn from itself, and the arguer is going round in circles.[1] Hence the fallacy is also known as arguing in a circle.

In high metaphysical arguments on ultimate questions one has to assume something, or one might never get

---

[1] See above, p. 116 ff. or discussion of the circularity of the syllogism in general.

started, and in those regions of thought it is hard to avoid all circularity.   Indeed a philosopher once said that arguing in a circle does not much matter, provided your circle is big enough.   However that may be, in ordinary arguments between man and man on human affairs, begging the question or arguing in a circle is a grave defect that may render the whole train of reasoning worthless.   If we assume what requires proof, we are just beggars, *begging* what we ought to *earn* by proof.   Here is a typical, though rather complex case, taken from life.

The Northumbrian theory of Early Christian art is that the Irish missionaries arrived in Northumbria without any art of their own, and learned their art, including their superb art of illuminating copies of Holy Scripture, from their Northumbrian converts.   The fine copy of the Gospels, known as the Book of Durrow, is a difficulty on the theory; for Durrow is in the centre of Ireland. The Book of Durrow is not known ever to have been out of Ireland in ancient days; its true title is Irish; its script is Irish; Irish names, Patrick and Columba, occur on its colophon page.   The Northumbrian theory has to *assume* that this ancient manuscript was written in Northumbria, as indeed it may have been.   But assumption is not proof.   Now here is the point of the illustration.   If the Book of Durrow *was* written in Northumbria, it could hardly be older than *c.* 690 A.D.; for Northumbria was too unsettled at an earlier date.   Therefore the Northumbrian theory has to assign it to a relatively late date, though it contains strong indications of having been written at an early date.   Step by step the theory is built up round the twin assumptions that the Book of Durrow is of late date and was written in Northumbria.   Then one day some art critic, not familiar with all the 'if's' in the case, jumps from assumption to proof, begs the question, and writes, ' Since the Book of Durrow was written *c.* 700 in Northumbria, it is strong confirmation of the Northumbrian theory of Irish art.' It may be so, but we do not prove such things by assuming them. Logic prescribes suspense of judgment and hypothetical, not categorical, propositions in all cases where proof is wanting.

(5) *Non Causa pro Causa*, or False Cause. This fallacy consists in assigning as the cause of an event what is not the cause, or in tracing a conclusion to a premiss with which it has no connection. Farmers traditionally connect changes in the weather with the quarters of the moon ; and superstition has attributed all sorts of causal properties to the Gulf Stream, and in recent times to the atomic bomb. A very common variety of False Cause is the fallacy, known as *Post hoc ; ergo propter hoc*, which means—After this, therefore, because of this, e.g. ' I walked under the ladder, and then left my gloves in the bus. Things like that always happen to me when I walk under ladders. It is very strange, and I cannot explain it ; but there must be some connection.'

(6) Consequent. The fallacy of the Consequent consists in treating the condition and its consequence as interchangeable, as is done frequently in the case of the hypothetical syllogism (see above, p. 148) where men argue illegitimately from the truth of the consequent to the truth of the antecedent, or from the falsity of the antecedent to the falsity of the consequent. Aristotle also applies the corresponding notion to terms. Water is necessarily wet, and man is necessarily animal ; *wet* and *animal* are consequents ; but if we treat them as interchangeable with their ' antecedents ' and argue that everything wet is water,

and all animals men, we are guilty of the fallacy of Consequent.

(7) *Many Questions.* The fallacy lies, not so much in asking several questions at once, as in trying to answer them all at once. It might well be called the Fallacy of the Single Answer. When the question is compound, we must not try to answer it as if it were single. Only a simpleton will give a single (Yes or No) answer to the stock question, Have you left off beating your Mother? For both *Yes* and *No* incriminate the answerer. Have you half-a-crown? Will you lend me half-a-crown? Those are two separate questions. Have you half-a-crown to lend me? That combines the two questions into the outward form of one; but it is one *compound* question that requires, and usually receives, a *compound* answer.

There are questions, simple in the asking, that become compound in the answering. Is Mrs. Smith at home? If I ask that question, I want to be told whether she is in the house, and if so, whether she is receiving, and if so, whether she will receive me.

Then there are questions that, in lawyers' language, are void for uncertainty. Do you dig with the right foot? Do you hold the right views on compost heaps? One is not bound to answer such questions; but a pinch of commonsense with one's logic will usually indicate the right reply. From Biblical days the ' subtle question ' has been a means of entangling people in their talk, and scrupulous fairness in framing and asking questions, as well as logical exactitude in answering them, are marks of the fair and disciplined mind.

Questions and Exercises on Chapter VIII

1. Define Enthymeme, and give instances.

2. Explain the structure of a Sorites, and state and prove the rules that govern it.

3. What are the *pros* and *cons* of calling Hypothetical and Disjunctive reasonings *syllogisms* ?

4. Give an instance of *Pure* Hypothetical syllogism.

5. Explain the construction of the ordinary Hypothetical syllogism. Name its two moods. Give instances of each, and state the rules of Inference and non-Inference.

6. Determine the structure of the Disjunctive syllogism. What is the ambiguity that haunts it ? Is it useful ? Give concrete instances of its moods, and discuss their validity.

7. Define Dilemma, and describe its main varieties. What are the historic names for answers to dilemmas ? Specify one of the famous Greek dilemmas.

8. What is a Fallacy ? What recurrent fallacies in categorical syllogisms have recognized names ? Give instances of each.

9. Describe the scope of Aristotle's lists of fallacies.

10. Give instances of Equivocation and Amphiboly.

11. The Fallacy of *Secundum Quid* is particularly subtle and dangerous.

12. An *Argumentum ad hominem* means two distinct things. Is it necessarily a fallacy ? How does it link up with *Ignoratio Elenchi* ?

13. What is *Begging the Question* ?

14. The Fallacy of *Many Questions* is more properly that of the *Single Answer*. Explain, and give examples.

CHAPTER IX

INDUCTION AND SCIENTIFIC METHOD

A COMMON sight in the days of the horse-drawn tram was a trace-horse, hitched to the tram at the approach to a steep incline. Induction, as originally conceived by Aristotle, was a trace-horse, or auxiliary process, designed to help the syllogism in its difficulty about the universal or general premiss. Subsequently Induction has broadened out, and has become a Logic in its own right, or a branch of Logic, but it still retains something of its original character as a supplement to the Logic of the syllogism, an annexe, as it were, of the main building.

By derivation Induction means *a leading on*, as Deduction means *a leading down from*. As a logical process Induction leads the mind on from fact to fact, like a working bee passing from flower to flower;[1] while Deduction, like the spider, draws down thread from thread, and weaves its web. The two processes meet at the General Proposition. Deduction must have general propositions to serve as premisses, and Induction can supply the need, or go some way towards it. To that extent Deductive Logic, the Logic of the Syllogism, and Inductive Logic, the Logic of Discovery, are complementary disciplines. They are certainly not in opposition; Induction has to make use of some deductive methods, while Deduction counts on Induction for many of its premisses.

The main business of Induction is to lead on from the particular to the general. Generalizations are its concern.

[1] Bacon, *Novum Organum*, I, 95.

Induction formulates rules for discovering generalizations, for testing and justifying them. Induction is specially interested in those generalizations we call Causes, and is of special importance in the work of science. Inductive Logic has left its mark on scientific tradition, and has contributed not a little to the long-established procedure, practised in our laboratories and known as Scientific Method.

Aristotle's Induction

Aristotle *intended* his Induction to be *Induction by Complete Enumeration*, and as an illustration of his meaning he gave what is known as the *Inductive Syllogism*:

> Man, horse, mule, etc. live long.
> Man, horse, mule, etc. are gall-less.
> ∴ The gall-less animals live long.[1]

The conclusion is to be understood universally, and it is valid, if and only if, the enumeration of the gall-less animals is complete. This is where the shoe pinches; for it is virtually impossible to make such an enumeration complete, and in consequence Bacon styled the Aristotelian process 'simple enumeration', implying that it was incomplete. If we were content to take the conclusion as an enumerative proposition, it would mean no more than 'All these gall-less animals live long', and that would not be a true universal or general proposition; we could not use it as a basis for inference or establish by it any causal connection between longevity and the absence of the gall; for short-lived gall-less animals might be discovered. Aristotle, of course, was alive to

[1] There is in fact no connection between longevity and the possession of the gall-bladder.

the difficulty. As a keen observer of nature, who himself experimented in biology in a small way, he knew that even an incomplete enumeration could be a useful collection of scientific facts; but as a logician he could not fail to know that an enumerative conclusion could be known to be true only of the specimens examined. That is why, of course, he insisted that Induction must be by *Complete* Enumeration.

The *Inductive Syllogism* has long been a target for criticism; for it appears to be looking one way and going the opposite way, like a man rowing a boat. But we must remember that Aristotle did not put it forward as expressing a full account of Induction, and that it does express well *part* of the process, namely that bee-like flower-to-flower and fact-to-fact movement of thought which is the beginning and the middle of Induction, but not its goal.

Take a homely modern instance. Mr. Jones installs a ' domestic boiler ', of the best type, mechanically perfect. It does its job and gives every satisfaction. In five years time, however, the *chimney* begins to give trouble; cracks occur; plaster falls; stains show on ceilings and walls; rooms must be re-decorated; and finally the chimney is taken down and re-built. Mr. Jones's case does not stand alone; similar cases are reported from all over the country. There is nothing wrong with the boiler *per se*; there is nothing wrong with the chimney when used for an open fire; but chimney defects occur when the boiler is installed. The Ministry of Housing appoints a research department to deal with the problem. Inductive methods are used; the trouble is traced to *internal* damp; the cure is found, when the cause is established. The true generalization *began* to take shape in the minds of the researchers when they passed from Mr. Jones's defective chimney to that of Mr. Smith, and the others, and found that 'All these defective chimneys were boiler chimneys, and liable to internal damp.'

Clearly then the mind of man does generalize along the lines indicated by the *Inductive Syllogism*, even though the completeness of the enumeration is an ideal, rarely realized. But was Aristotle right in saying that we arrive at our first principles by a process of Induction?[1]   He was, provided we do not take these words of his to mean that the enumeration of instances is enough by itself. He was thinking of the whole complex process of Induction, not of part. It is not wise to trace our principles and generalizations, be they homely or scientific, to any one source; some of them are born of experience, some are dictates of reason; some are bred in the bone; some are inferences; some have a basis in vital instinct and some in intellectual intuition. Aristotle was just the man to appreciate the mixed character of our principles, and the varied sources of our generalizations and premisses. He believed in reason, and he believed in experience; he was a realist about sensible experience, and yet his mind moved easily in geometry and the other deductive sciences. Now geometry supplies the clue that explains his attitude to Induction; for in geometry we never actually *see* the triangles and other figures about which we reason so confidently. We *see* very thin lines, possessing *some* breadth and *almost* straight, and triangles *approximately* isosceles; those approximations set us thinking about the ideal figures and properties of space. Similarly Induction, as an observation and enumeration of the individual facts of nature, was for Aristotle a process that *awoke* thought, and 'led on' to the general proposition. He wished Induction to be

[1] See *Analytica Posteriora*, II, 19, 100b.

'Perfect Induction' resting on an ideally Complete Enumeration; but he knew that in practice we have to be content with less. Broadly, he viewed Inductive Logic as a supplementary discipline, required by the limitations of Syllogistic Logic, and he saw Induction as a systematic, if imperfect, collection of scientific facts, as complete as each case permits, to be followed by a leap of intuition (Greek, νοῦς), by which we see with the mind's eye the laws of nature, exemplified in particular instances, as the geometer sees with his mind's eye the laws of space exemplified in the imperfect figures of space, which he draws on paper or traces in the sand.

Bacon's Criticism

Francis Bacon (1561–1626) criticized severely the Logic of his day. It does more harm than good, he said; for the syllogism is "no match for the subtlety of nature. It commands assent therefore to the proposition, but does not take hold of the thing . . . Our only hope therefore lies in a true induction." That he had Aristotelian induction in mind here is shown by the following quotation, "The induction which proceeds by simple enumeration is childish; its conclusions are precarious, and exposed to peril from a contradictory instance; and it generally decides on too small a number of facts, and on those only which are at hand. But the induction which is to be available for the discovery and demonstration of sciences and arts, must analyse nature by proper rejections and exclusions." [1]

It is easier to pull down than to build. Bacon's own Inductive method is hard to understand, and has never

Bacon, *Novum Organum*, I, 12–14, 105.

been widely used. It is contained in an incomplete form in the second Book of his *Novum Organum*. It is an impracticable search for ' Forms ', and is of little account today. Bacon's lasting contributions to logic lie elsewhere. They are, (1) His cutting attack on an unbalanced cult of the syllogism. (2) His refusal to rest content with mere tradition, and his inspiring call for reform in Logic and for a ' true induction '. (3) His insistence on ' the negative instance ', and on the ' rejections and exclusions ', which anticipate Mill's methods, to which we now pass.

Mill's Inductive Logic

Of later writers on Induction the most influential is John Stuart Mill (1806-73). His general line is to play up inductive Logic and to play down deductive. He denies that he feels contempt for the syllogism, but as is clear from the discussion above (pp. 116-23) on its alleged circularity, he assigns it an inferior rôle. From the syllogism Mill passes straight to the general proposition, saying of it, " Not only *may* we reason from particulars to particulars without passing through generals, but we perpetually do so reason. All our earliest inferences are of this nature ... The child, who, having burnt his fingers, avoids to thrust them again into the fire, has reasoned or inferred, though he has never thought of the general maxim, Fire burns." [1]

They are striking words, and they bring out the important point that the question about the syllogism and its premisses is bound up with the broader question, How do we get our general notions and general propositions? One could argue about the burnt child till the cows come

[1] J. S. Mill, *op. cit.*, Book II, iii, 3.

home, and be no nearer agreement. Of course the child does not *consciously* think of general maxims; but who is to say that he does not all the same think of the general properties of fire, and register a general note to that effect in his subconscious mind? After all, the burnt child dreads *the* fire, not this fire and that fire alone, but *the* fire, fire in general, and he has not learned his lesson if he dreads only the particular fire that burnt him. The general judgment, *Fire burns*, is there in his mind, even if the general maxim has not yet found expression by his lips. The moth with singed wing dipping again and again into the flame is symbolic of the man who goes (it is supposed) from particular to particular, and never puts two and two together. The reactions of moth or unconscious babe are neither here nor there; but it is extremely doubtful whether a grown man, or even a child, could in any true meaning of the words 'reason from particulars to particulars without passing through generals'. If he *reasons*, the minimum requirement is the perception of similarity in the cases, and a particular conceived as a similar is no longer perceived in its particularity, but is conceived as an instance of a general, expressed or implied. Mill's words, quoted above, have been very influential, but they beg a big question.

Mill defines Induction as " the operation of discovering and proving general propositions ". He is at pains to point out that propositions that merely sum up a number of particular cases or that merely bind several facts together in one statement are not properly called inductions; here he has in mind Aristotle's Induction by enumeration; he held that piling up instances is not enough, and he called it a ' mystery ' why in some cases a single instance will suffice to establish a general proposition, while in other cases a thousand instances will not do so.

Mill's next step is to bring his logic into close touch with the external world of things, making our mental processes run in double harness, as it were, with natural process, and almost equating general propositions with laws of nature.

Behind all our generalizations about the world there is, he says, one primary assumption, viz. the uniformity of nature. That day will follow night, and night, day, that the seasons of the year will take their accustomed course, that fruit trees will bud, and blossom, and bear fruit, and shed their leaves, and begin the cycle all over again—we rarely give these sequences a second thought for they are all part of that great consistent pattern of events that we call uniformity of nature, or the natural order. The uniformity of nature is itself an induction, and cannot explain our inductions ; and we have only to look at the evidences of the ice age to realize that much that we now regard as part of the natural order was not always so ; but the conception of, at least, a relative uniformity and order lies behind our inductions, and Mill calls it ' the general principle ' of Induction.

Elaborating his theme, Mill is led to the notion of a grand uniformity made up of lesser uniformities, each of which is called a law of nature. Thus the search for the laws of nature becomes (in Mill's words), " the search for the fewest and simplest assumptions which being granted the whole existing order would follow ".

Bodies unsupported fall. Hot air rises. Water seeks its own level. Water quenches fire. Fire burns wood. Sown seed grows. The sun will rise and set tomorrow. These general propositions with hundreds more like them we all accept, and use as major premises for thought and action. It matters little what we call them, and they answer to different names in different contexts. They are uniformities ; they are laws of nature ; they are primary assumptions ; they are major premises ; they are master-inductions. Whatever name we give them, they are sign-posts to knowledge, leading to an ordered view of an orderly universe. Inductive logic draws our attention to them, makes us familiar with them, grateful for them, and yet somewhat critical of them.

One would like to think that Induction had succeeded in helping the tram to top the rise. But, alas, the trace-horse itself sometimes can hardly keep its feet on the slippery slope. There is nothing radically wrong with either part of Logic, but both parts have to work with something less than absolute certainty. And they are none the worse, but all the better for that. Moral cer-tainty and relative assurance are in keeping with man's powers of mind and his station in the scheme of things. One hundred years ago, and less, Newton's Laws were regarded as Gospel truth, and the skies would fall, men thought, if those laws came down. Well, they have come down in rank and status, and the skies have not fallen, and the build-up of knowledge goes on. Major premises, whether ' deduced ' or ' induced ', together with laws of nature and general propositions of all sorts, should be ' kept in solution ', that is, should be kept supple and elastic, and not allowed to harden off; then they can be revised from time to time, and kept in touch with the growth of knowledge.

After discussing general propositions and premises Mill transposes his theme into a different key. He passes to the allied search for causes, writing, " To ascertain, therefore, what are the laws of causation which exist in nature; to determine the effect of every cause, and the causes of all effects—is the main business of Induction; and to point out how this is done is the chief object of Inductive Logic." [1]

Mill leaves efficient causes almost entirely on one side; his Logic is not concerned with causes that actually make changes begin to be. He understands cause and effect in terms of *before*, *after*, and *necessity*. A *cause*, for him, is the invariable and unconditional antecedent of the phenomenon, and an *effect* is its invariable and unconditional consequent. Such 'causes' are important for Logic, as well as for science. They are signs whose connection with the thing signified really is invariable and necessary; and thus they form the material of the general propositions we seek.

In the search for such signs or causes the two main aids are the method of Observation and the method of Experiment. A brief comment must be made on each method. They are not, of course, completely separate, and they can work together in harmony, sometimes one, sometimes the other, leading the way.

Observation means much more than a casual glance, or two. Observation must be systematic, continued, discriminating, and comprehensive, and needless to say, it must be honest. As often as not a whole network of antecedents precedes the phenomenon in question, some relevant, some not. A trained observer will distinguish one antecedent from another, will note the relevant and disregard the rest. The quality of the observation can make a great difference to its results. Superficial observation may hide the cause, and not reveal it. Here is an

[1] J. S. Mill, *op. cit.*, Book III, vi. 3.

instance from the lighter side of life. The angler observes that trout often, but by no means always, *take* just before the rain, when the first few drops strike the surface of the river or lake. What is the cause? One's first instinct is to attribute it to the rain itself, as freshening the stale water. But if so, why does it not always happen? Why does the rain sometimes have the diametrically opposite effect? Sometimes the rain puts the trout off the feed, and may put them down for the rest of the day. Observation has to look at the phenomenon with discrimination; for it has a network of antecedents. Many things condition the movements and the appetite of trout, and they must all be considered. The force and direction of the wind, the temperature of the water, the temperature of the air, the colour on the water, the pattern, dressing and size of the artificial fly—all these must be observed intelligently and passed in review; but they do not appear to have any special connection with our phenomenon. It is not the rain itself; for cold, driving, long-continued rain does not produce the phenomenon; it is an accompanying circumstance of warm, soft, intermittent, summery rain, which brings the trout up because it brings the fly and midge down, along with the swallows, from the upper air, and strews the surface of the lake with food. Only in that sense is the rain the 'cause' of the catch; it is a sign to the trout to expect a fall of food, as it is a sign to the angler to expect a rise of trout.

Experiment, as everyone knows, is the central feature of many sciences, and the principal instrument of scientific discovery. In one sense every meal cooked is an experiment; but the essence of scientific experiment lies in 'varying the circumstances' (in Bacon's phrase). By *varying the circumstances* the phenomenon in question can sometimes be reproduced with a difference, and that can be done accurately only under laboratory conditions. To repeat the phenomenon and vary it under controlled and measured conditions is the surest way of ascertaining its 'invariable and unconditional antecedent', and thus testing hypotheses and proving general propositions.

Take the case of a geologist interested in a bed of coarse sand rock formed on the floor of the ocean. He wants to know how such coarse sand can be carried far into the ocean deep, and what gives rise to the features which distinguish it from sands deposited in shallow water. He wants to determine the causes and conditions and be in a position to make sound and solid generalizations. He observes with a trained eye similar deposits of past oceans which have been heaved up to form the land of the present time. From these observations he forms a hypothesis that the coarse sands were carried into the oceans by fast-moving, turbulent currents of muddy water called turbidity currents, which originated from swollen rivers or from avalanches on the steep ocean margins.

How can he test such a hypothesis? He cannot experiment directly. The chemist can place substances in test-tubes and subject them to analysis. But there is no experimenting with swollen rivers or the bed of the ocean. He cannot watch turbidity currents there nor vary the conditions and circumstances. But he can experiment indirectly: he can experiment with models; he can construct in miniature in his own back garden a segment of an ocean floor. He can launch turbidity currents, can vary the slope of the ocean floor, the density and coarseness of the mixture, can watch and measure the speed of the current at any distance from its source, can measure the deposit of sand and the patterns of current erosion at its

G

base which he is trying to explain. In such a case, if the scaling and calculations were accurately done, the geologist's hypothesis could be tested, and verified general propositions about the turbidity currents in his back garden could be reasonably extended to the action of turbidity currents on the bed of the ocean.

Mill's system of Experimental Methods

There are sciences where from the nature of the case hypothesis and experiment can play only a very minor part. When scientific information is required, for instance, by a Department of Agriculture on the growth or marketing of soft fruit, experiment would be desired; but experiments with crops in the open air can rarely be as exact and conclusive as laboratory experiments. It is a widely held belief that strawberry beds containing mixed varieties are more liable to virus disease than those containing but one variety; but to prove it conclusively by experiment would be difficult and costly. Now in such cases where actual experiment in the laboratory or in the open air is impracticable, a knowledge of Mill's system of Experimental Methods is invaluable; for familiarity with his Methods ensures that at least the spirit of the laboratory and of Scientific Method, with its insistence on rigorous proof, will be carried into our other reasonings.

Mill elaborated five Methods, each with its Canon or Rule, and they were probably intended as an inductive counterpart to the figures and moods of the syllogism. Mill makes high claims for them, maintaining that no scientific truth was ever established without them. The five Methods between them constitute a code of principles of investigation which has always commanded attention and respect, and which undoubtedly is an important contribution to scientific method. They are more useful perhaps in eliminating error than in finding truth; but they have a general correspondence with the mind's instinctive procedure when we are in doubt about a supposed case of causal relationship. When we are in doubt as to whether A is the cause of B, we take similar cases, AB, aB, Ab, etc.; we study the points of agreement; we study the points of difference; we study the agreements *plus* differences; we study residual factors and concomitant variations. Those five lines of study are the principles, respectively, of Mill's Five Methods. Here are his Methods, expressed in the form of Rules, with his Instances in outline.

The Rule of Agreement

If two or more instances of the phenomenon under investigation have only one circumstance in common, the circumstance in which alone all the instances agree is the cause (or effect) of the given phenomenon.

What is the cause of crystallization? The instances in which bodies assume crystalline structure may have no other point of agreement; but they have one circumstance in common, viz. the deposition of a solid matter from a liquid state. That circumstance is therefore the invariable antecedent and the cause. N.B. It is not wise to study Agreements and overlook Differences.

The Rule of Difference

If an instance in which the phenomenon under investigation occurs, and an instance in which it does not occur, have every circumstance in common save one, that one occurring only in the former, the circumstance in which alone the two instances differ,

*is the effect, or the cause, or an indispensable part of the cause,
of the phenomenon.*

If a man is shot through the heart, he dies, and the gun-shot was the cause. It is the same man I saw and talked to yesterday, same features, same coloured hair, same clothes, same flower in buttonhole. Then he was alive and whole and talking and bursting with energy. Now he is dead and still and silent, and there is a gaping wound in his left side. It was not old age or poison or a stroke. The wound with the shot that made it is the cause.

The Rule of Agreement and Difference (' The Joint Method ')

*If two or more instances in which the phenomenon occurs have
only one circumstance in common, while two or more instances
in which it does not occur have nothing in common save the absence
of that circumstance ; the circumstance in which alone the two
sets of instances differ, is the effect, or the cause, or an indispensable part of the cause, of the phenomenon.*

What is the cause of dew? Mill replies with a long, methodical, and subtle discussion.[1] He begins with a preliminary operation, which he names ' abstraction ', to determine what exactly is meant by *dew*. It is not rain nor the moisture of fogs, but the moisture that appears on things exposed in the open air when no rain or visible wet is falling.

Are there any similar phenomena ? Yes ; they are, (1) the moisture on a cold metal or stone when we breathe on it, (2) that which appears on a glass of water fresh from the well in hot weather, (3) that which appears on windows and windscreens when there is cold rain or hail outside, (4) the sweat on walls indoors in a warm thaw after a long

---

[1] From Sir John Herschel's *Discourse on the Study of Natural Philosophy*, and Dr. Wells' theory of dew.

frost. All these instances, similar to dew, agree in the coldness of the thing on which the dew appears. Does this hold of nocturnal dew? Yes, though at first one might think otherwise. Place a thermometer on the be-dewed thing, and another thermometer a little above it. Invariably the bedewed thing is found to be colder. Thus by the Method of Agreement we have established a causal connection between dew and the coldness of the bedewed thing; but we have not found out which is cause and which is effect, nor whether both the dew and the cold are the effects of something else.

We must therefore turn to the Method of Difference; we must collect more facts, and we must 'vary the circumstances'.

No dew is produced on polished metals, but it is pro-duced copiously on plates of glass. Here are our two differing instances; but we cannot yet be sure that the latter instance agrees with the former in every circum-stance but one. All we know so far is that the cause of dew will be found among the circumstances that distin-guish the glass plates from the polished metals.

Various types of polished surfaces are then studied. It is found that those are most strongly bedewed that conduct heat worst. Good conductors resist dew. The deposition of dew must therefore be in some proportion to the body's power of resisting the passage of heat. Then substitute roughened surfaces for polished, and it is found that the surface as well as the material is concerned. Roughened iron, especially when painted or blackened, bedews sooner than varnished paper. Surfaces that radiate their heat most readily contract dew most copiously. Texture is then studied. Stones, metals, and things of firm texture do not bedew easily; but loose-textured things, such as wool,[1] velvet, and cloth bedew easily. Looseness of texture is therefore causally connected with the deposition of dew. But this cause resolves itself into the first; for substances of loose texture are used for clothing just because they hinder the passage of heat from the skin to the air. The one induction corroborates the other. The instances of great deposit of dew agree in this, and in this only, that they either radiate heat rapidly or conduct it slowly, and therefore the body tends to lose heat from the surface more rapidly than it can be restored from within.

The Rule of Residues

Subduct from any phenomenon such part as is known by previous inductions to be the effect of certain antecedents, and the residue of the phenomenon is the effect of the remaining antecedents.

The Method of Residues is a modification of the Method of Difference. It is an important way of investigating nature. Examine, it says, what everyone else throws away.[2] Inquiry into the cause of sound left a residual velocity unaccounted for. Laplace suggested that this velocity might arise from the heat developed in the act of condensation which takes place at every vibration by which sound is conveyed.

---

[1] It is of some interest to note that a woollen fleece was used in the earliest recorded experiment with dew (Judges vi *ad fin.*). To test his 'call' Gideon exposed a fleece of wool; next morning he wrung a bowl of dew out of it, though the ground was dry. He tried the same experiment next night, and the following morning the situation was reversed; the fleece was dry, and all the ground around it was wet with dew. The ancient Semites, as dwellers in tents, were naturally interested in the problem of dew, and the story of Gideon looks as if they knew something about the Method of Difference.

[2] Cf. the discovery of penicillin by the late Sir Alexander Fleming.

The Rule of Concomitant Variations

Whatever phenomenon varies in any manner whenever another phenomenon varies in some particular manner, is either a cause or an effect of that phenomenon, or is connected with it through some fact of causation.

The chief use of this method is for dealing with cases involving the 'Permanent Causes', which we cannot remove; e.g. the sun, earth, air, etc. As the position of the moon varies, there are corresponding variations in the time and place of high water, and as the place is always the part of the earth which is nearest to the moon, or that which is most remote from it, the moon is wholly or partially the cause which determines the tides.

It is scarcely necessary to add that the student who wishes to make an adequate study of Induction and Scientific Method must go far beyond the contents of this present work. All that was possible here within the space available was a sketch of the historical landmarks in Inductive Logic, introducing its leading themes. Other topics requiring attention and dealt with in all treatises on Induction are :

(*a*) Explanation. What is the nature of Explanation ? What are its aims, methods, and limits ? How does scientific explanation differ from historical explanation ? When is a phenomenon scientifically explained ? How does the 'Deductive Method of Induction' (as Mill called it) enter into Explanation ?

(*b*) Theories and Hypotheses. Their construction and verification. The planning and execution of research.

(*c*) Scientific Certainty. In what does it consist ?

(*d*) Cause and Effect. What do the words mean ? What are the Causal Laws ? Whole volumes have been written on this subject. It is a case in which Logic soon passes over into philosophy.

CHAPTER X

SYMBOLIC LOGIC

SYMBOLIC Logic is a comparatively recent development of logical studies. About one hundred years old, it has grown rapidly, and is still growing. Its aims have varied from time to time, and in different countries it has taken different forms. As taught at present in the British Isles, it has an elastic programme, and its symbols in use at the earlier stages are standardized; at the higher stages for the specialist it appears to contain the possibility of almost unlimited expansion with a correspondingly wide range of symbols. The following notes are for the novice who wishes to know what Symbolic Logic is about, something of its history, and how it differs from Aristotelian Logic.

The Logic set out in the previous pages is a compact and standardized body of doctrine, two thousand years old and more. It is deeply rooted in our language, and our language is deeply rooted in it. It has its defects and its limitations, but it contains something for everybody; and it is relatively easy to learn and easy to teach. In twenty to thirty lectures a good lecturer can teach the bones of it to any co-operative student of university standing. A student teaching himself may require a rather longer period; but after two to three months' study he should feel at home in it. When he has mastered the structure of the syllogism and the Rules of the Figures, he ought to be in a position to take stock and judge his own aptitude for the subject. If then he feels an aptitude for Logic and an interest in its deeper aspects, let him open a textbook on elementary Symbolic Logic, and try his hand at it.

The two Logics

The mathematically-minded are likely to be attracted. Symbolic Logic is mathematical in origin, and mathematical in technique and method. It is also known as Mathematical Logic, or as Logistic[1]; for it is concerned with the logic of mathematics, as well as with the mathematics of Logic. Its relation to Aristotelian Logic is complex and difficult to describe briefly. The two Logics are in competition; they are in opposition; they are complementary. There is truth in all three statements, but no one of them fully meets the case. The older symbolists were strongly critical of the Aristotelian tradition, and preferred to be independent of it. The present tendency is to look on Aristotle as the founder of both Logics, and to speak of Symbolic Logic as a later development from the earlier. There were developments in Logic in ancient times after the death of Aristotle, especially among the Stoics, and what has been taught as Aristotle's has not always been what Aristotle taught; but the evidence for any historic connection between Aristotle and modern Symbolic Logic is slight. From the learner's point of view the two Logics are different disciplines, dealing with rather different aspects of human discourse. The relation between Aristotelian Logic and Symbolic Logic is not unlike that between arithmetic and algebra. Arithmetic and algebra both speak of quantity; but to the beginner, at any rate, they speak in different languages.

Many of the semi-grammatical distinctions, traditionally

---

[1] From the Greek λογιστική, the science of calculation.

taught by Logic, are of little interest to the symbolist; but on the other hand he studies carefully particles and connecting links which the traditional Logic tends to take for granted. On the syllogism and the proposition the two Logics take different views. The symbolist regards the syllogism as a relatively unimportant mode of inference, one amongst many, and the proposition as a statement of a relation between two or more terms, and not necessarily a predication. Thus the symbolist can look at discourse from the wider angle and can treat of sentences and arguments that Aristotelian Logic has to leave on one side. This increased scope and range is not, however, all pure gain. It is certainly of interest to know that sentences, not in subject-predicate form, or only imperfectly so, are capable of logical treatment; but there is much to be said for the old view that if a man has an important contribution to make to knowledge, he will almost certainly predicate, that is, he will assert or deny a predicate of a subject. It is also true that syllogistic inference has a position of importance in the build-up of knowledge, and as a reasoner's training-ground.

Attempts have been made to combine the two Logics into one; but the results have not been altogether satisfactory. High theory apart, from the practical standpoint of the learner, the two disciplines are different, and belong to different stages of development. The one can learn from the other, of course; they can combine in that sense, but it is doubtful whether they can be unified without loss to both. Aristotelian Logic is an instrument of general culture, carried out in the vernacular. Symbolic Logic is a specialist study, which uses a specialist technique, of interest and importance to the mathematician and the professional logician. J. Venn, an eminent symbolist, who was the first to use the name *Symbolic Logic* in the title of a book, appears to have been of this opinion. He protested against the idea that Aristotelian Logic had been superseded as a branch of education, and maintained that it ought to be taught in the traditional way. He gave three reasons : (1) Some of the most instructive parts of common logic, such as connotation and denotation, definition, and the ordinary rules of conversion and opposition, do not come within the scope of Symbolic Logic. (2) Perfect clearness on these points is essential for accuracy, and is best acquired in the ordinary manuals. (3) Common Logic has the merit of close association with grammar and the ordinary forms of speech.[1]

Historical

In the long history of Logic many attempts have been made to improve the Aristotelian system, and to extend its range. Leibniz (1646–1716), the famous philosopher and mathematician, made such an attempt. He suggested that a universal language of ideograms[2] should be formed to express scientific concepts, and to make possible a universal calculus of reasoning. Both those notions reappear in Symbolic Logic ; but Leibniz himself did not carry his suggestion far, and it had no positive results.

A. de Morgan (1806–71) and G. Boole (1815–64) have both been named as founders of the school. They were both Professors of Mathematics, the former in University College, London, the latter in Queen's College, Cork. De Morgan wrote *Formal Logic or the Calculus of Inference*,

[1] J. Venn, *Symbolic Logic* (1881), p. xxvi.   [2] Picture signs.

London, 1847, and he developed and modified it in his *Syllabus of a Proposed System of Logic*, London, 1860. Boole's main works were, *Mathematical Analysis of Logic*, Cambridge, 1847, and *An Investigation of the Laws of Thought*, London, 1854. Both writers used new sets of symbols extensively. Boole aimed at determining the basic laws of reasoning, and at expressing them in the symbolic language of an algebraical calculus. He sought, in his own words, " equations interpretable as propositions ". His system, which was nearly complete, was based on new notions of the class, including that of the ' null class '. De Morgan's system was arithmetical. In the Preface of his *Syllabus* he says that his system was entirely based on " the *arithmetical* view of the proposition and syllogism ". The proposition is, he says, " the presentation, for assertion or denial, of two names connected by a relation ".[1] The first-mentioned name, the name in relation, is, he says, the subject ; the second name, the name to which it is in relation, is the predicate. He treated the syllogism on similar lines. A syllogism is valid, he says, when its conclusion contains one item of quantity for every unit-syllogism necessarily contained in the premisses. De Morgan's study of relations is influential still.

The influential Cambridge symbolist, J. Venn (1834–1923), has already been mentioned ; he made important contributions on existential import, on the logic of classes, and on implication, and he is remembered for his experiments in a propositional calculus, and for his diagrams.

A decisive stage in the history of Symbolic Logic was marked by the *Principia Mathematica* (1910) of A. N. Whitehead and Bertrand Russell. The earlier symbolists applied mathematics to Logic ; Whitehead and Russell applied

[1] *Syllabus*, p. 42.

Logic to mathematics. The earlier symbolists aimed at reforming Logic on the mathematical model, at correcting its errors, at freeing it from the yoke of Aristotle, and at reaching a universal calculus which would automatically settle the validity of an argument, or determine the degree of probability it possessed. Whitehead and Russell viewed the reform of Logic from the standpoint of mathematics; they studied its effects on the basic concepts of mathematics, and used the new Logic to set those concepts beyond criticism. In a later work, *An Introduction to Mathematical Philosophy* (1919), Lord Russell writes (p. 194) that both mathematics and logic " have developed in modern times; logic has become more mathematical and mathematics has become more logical. The consequence is that it has now become wholly impossible to draw a line between the two; in fact the two are one. They differ as boy and man; logic is the youth of mathematics and mathematics is the manhood of logic." That impressive statement by one who has been *pars magna* of the new movement deserves to be quoted; but it is only fair to add (for the comfort of those who are not mathematicians) that the words " in fact the two are one ", however true of mathematics and Symbolic Logic, could hardly be said of mathematics and Aristotelian Logic. Students understand Aristotelian Logic, and profit by it, who are perfectly innocent of mathematics, and who find Symbolic Logic very hard. For them ' the two ' are *two*. I think this needs to be said; for in the universities today the struggle for existence among the subjects of the *curricula* is keen. Logic has lost its former proud position of ' compulsory subject ', and is now fighting for a place among the ' optionals '. If it is to be identified with Mathematical Logic, its appeal will be confined to Honour students in mathematics, philosophy, and statistics; and the humanities and the professions will be the poorer.

Finally, a recent work of an independent character that cuts across the traditional lines must be mentioned. It is *Aristotle's Syllogistic from the standpoint of Modern Formal Logic* (Oxford, 1951), by the eminent Polish logician, Jan Lukasiewicz, who died recently. He held " that there is a fundamental difference between the Aristotelian and the traditional syllogism ", and that, apart from his own exposition " there does not exist today a trustworthy exposition of the Aristotelian syllogistic ". In his fourth chapter, using a symbolism of his own, he sets out to express Aristotle's system in symbolist form, and has " tried to complete this syllogistic on the lines laid down by Aristotle himself ".[1] It is an advanced work of singular erudition that corrects the traditional view of Aristotle on several points.

The Symbols

Symbolic Logic takes its name from its free and independent use of symbols. Symbols have great educational value; a good system of symbols constitutes a mental shorthand which enables much to be said in a small space. A *symbol* is something, e.g. a tally, that makes you think of something else. Letters of the alphabet are symbols, and so are words and figures; but we are so accustomed to them, and the mind passes so quickly from them to their meaning that we scarcely think of them as symbols. The word *symbol* today generally means an unusual sign, such as an ideogram. Ordinary symbols, as we have seen, are

[1] *Ibid.*, Preface.

in use in Aristotelian Logic, and serve an important purpose there ; but they are few in number, simple, and self-explanatory, and the average student takes them in his stride, and does not notice them as symbols. The symbols of Symbolic Logic are far more numerous, more complex, and they have a richer purpose. The symbols in Aristotelian Logic, like S, P, and M, or A, E, I, and O are optional ; they are an educational convenience, assisting memory and facilitating argument. The symbols of the symbolist are *that*, and a good deal more ; how much more is not easy to say ; for some symbolists, not all, have denied that symbols are essential to their work. However that may be, symbols are recognized as having this advantage over words, for the symbolist, viz. that they are an unusual medium, and thus they take the mind off the concrete realities suggested by words, and fix it on abstract forms, which can only with difficulty be expressed in words. Moreover some important principles of Symbolic Logic look trivial when expressed in words, and the use of symbols lessens their trivial appearance.

The symbols in general use in the British Isles today are, in the main, those advocated by Lord Russell ;[1] but some minor changes have been introduced into his system. They are the joy of some students, the despair of others. Students with mathematical abilities master them with ease, and find them helpful and interesting ; to some they are a hurdle to be surmounted, and some can make nothing of them.

The basic symbols in the propositional calculus in Russell's system are as follows : (*a*) for Propositional Variables, (*b*) for Logical Constants.

---

[1] Those used by Lukasiewicz (see above, p. 196) are completely different.

(*a*) Propositions are represented by the letters *p*, *q*, and *r*, which are called *Propositional Variables*, because they can stand for *any* propositions. Thus *p* can stand for ' Men must work ', ' Balbus built a wall ', ' Logic is worthy of study ', or any other statement that can be true or false.

(*b*) Contrasted with the Variables are the *Logical Constants*, which connect the Variables, and form *truth-functions*, as they are named in mathematical language. There are four fundamental logical constants, *not*, *and*, *or*, and *if . . . then*, with corresponding truth-functions. These constants yield

(1) *The Contradictory function*, symbolized by ' ∼ '. Thus ∼*p* negates *p*, and means that the proposition *p* is false. If *p* stands for ' Men must work ', then ∼*p* stands for its contradictory, ' Men must not work ', or ' It is false that men must work.' Then if *p* is true, ∼*p* is false ; and if *p* is false, ∼*p* is true.

(2) *The Conjunctive function*, symbolized by ' . '. Thus *p.q* stands for a compound sentence, like ' Men must work and women must weep', which is true if its component propositions are both true, and false if either or both are false.

(3) *The Disjunctive function*, symbolized by ' ∨ ', from the Latin *vel*. Thus *p* ∨ *q* means ' either *p* or *q* ', and stands for any disjunction, such as ' Men must either work or starve.' Now as we saw above (p. 59), the word *or* in English is ambiguous, and may be inclusive, like ' and/or ', or exclusive, like ' or, but not both '. Symbolists interpret *or* in the *inclusive* sense. Thus *p* ∨ *q* is true, except when *both p* and *q* are false. Some logicians use the sign ∧ to represent the *exclusive or*, and those who do so would mean by *p* ∧ *q* that if *p* is true, *q* is false, and that if *p* is false, *q* is true.

(4) *The Implicative function*, symbolized by the sign ⊃. Thus $p \supset q$ means, 'If p, then q', i.e. a hypothetical proposition, such as, 'If you lend me half-a-crown, I will pay you back next week'—which could be expressed in a round-about way as 'Your lending me half-a-crown *implies* my paying you back next week.' $p \supset q$ is true, except when p is true, and q false.

Truth-tables and Equivalence

Truth-tables are then formed for each truth-function. The symbols T and F, or 1 and 0 are used, respectively, for *true* and *false*. Examples :

p	q	$p \lor q$
T	T	T
T	F	T
F	T	T
F	F	F

p	q	$p \cdot q$
T	T	T
T	F	F
F	T	F
F	F	F

When two propositions have the same truth-value, they are said to be *equivalent* or *materially equivalent*. This difficult notion is represented by the symbol ≡, a variation of the familiar sign of equality.

Punctuation

The foregoing symbols for constants and variables require punctuation when the system is worked out, and logical punctuation is supplied by a system of parentheses and brackets, or, in some systems, by strokes.

Other sets of Symbols

The symbols of the Propositional Calculus, outlined above, are fundamental; they are carried forward into the further developments of the system. New sets of symbols are brought in, as they are required. For instance, in the Predicate Calculus the letters *a*, *b*, and *c* are used for proper names, as *individual constants*, and the letters *f*, *g*, and *h*, as *predicate constants*; and singular propositions are symbolized by such combinations as *fa*, *ga*, *fb*, etc. The treatment of Existential Propositions and the Class Calculus gives rise to further sets of symbols.

The student will see from the above sketch that he must be prepared for something like learning a foreign language. Indeed the first steps in Symbolic Logic are inevitably an exercise in translating from the mother tongue with all its elasticity and wealth of suggestion and risk of ambiguity into a rigorous scientific language of symbols of a mathematical character. With practice, however, the unfamiliar medium becomes as simple and suggestive, as, say, *zero* or the *plus* and *minus* signs.

Aims and Programmes

What does Symbolic Logic teach, and aim at teaching? Full and final answers to these questions are hard to come by. Answers adequate yesterday and today might not be true tomorrow. Philosophers find it hard to say what philosophy teaches at any given time, let alone what it will teach tomorrow. Eminent mathematicians have said much the same about the higher mathematics. You must enter the water before you can learn to swim; and the proverb is true of Logic, both for those who teach it, and those who learn. It is especially true of a comparatively new subject, like Symbolic Logic; we must make a start on it before we take our bearings in it, and we must go some way in it before we can forecast its future developments.

It is, however, safe to say that Symbolic Logic does not work to any cut-and-dried programme or with hard-and-fast aims. Even at the elementary level there is no programme, universally agreed, or course of study, comparable in fixity to that of the elementary Logic of tradition. At the higher levels in both disciplines the doors of the future remain wide open, and the directions taken by logical studies will be decided, as in the past, by the leaders of logical thought, interpreting the cultural needs of their day.

Textbooks on Symbolic Logic in the last half-century have differed considerably in their contents and arrangement, and in their spirit and outlook. Some have been more philosophical, some more mathematical; some have been more concerned with theory, and some with practice. One opens with a chapter on the nature of thought, and ends with a chapter on the nature of the universe. One is occupied with the deducing of a chain of speculative principles, connected like the propositions and theorems of Euclidean geometry. One plunges straight into propositional analysis and a sea of symbols. Then there are textbooks that share the aims of Aristotelian Logic, that deal with common difficulties in higher grammar, that keep close to the logic of discourse and the inferences and reasonings of common life.

This mixture of aims and diversity of programme traces in large part to its history. Symbolic Logic originated in connection with mathematical theory and Aristotelian

Logic, the connection in the latter case being that of critical opposition. Having these twin roots, Symbolic Logic naturally gives teaching on (*a*) the logic of mathematics, (*b*) Aristotelian Logic, and (*c*) makes its own contribution to the logic of discourse.

For its teaching on the logic of mathematics the student should refer to the monumental classic, already mentioned, *Principia Mathematica* by Whitehead and Russell. Involving a close study of the primary concepts of mathematics, it is a very advanced work, almost entirely for specialists.

What Symbolic Logic teaches about Aristotelian Logic and its manner of teaching have varied considerably from time to time. Common to all its expositors is the claim that Symbolic Logic covers the same ground as Aristotelian Logic, but goes much further afield ; and it seems to be taken for granted that Symbolic Logic cannot be taught without some reference to Aristotelian Logic. The latter Logic appears to be required as a springboard, if not as a basis. At first symbolists were content to supplement tradition ; they left it to conservative logicians to teach the old Logic, and themselves came in with their additional teaching, correcting mistakes of the old Logic, widening its outlook, and dispelling the narrow cult of the syllogism. This was a fair and natural division of labour between the two schools of thought, which enriched the common stock ; for valuable discussions of existential import, class-membership propositions, and similar topics were added—to the benefit of both Logics. The two Logics existed side by side, much in the same way as Deductive Logic and Inductive Logic had done. The period of peaceful co-existence was interrupted when symbolists asked, Why have two Logics, or three ? Why

not have only one? Accordingly they have tried the
experiment of teaching Aristotelian Logic in textbooks
of Symbolic Logic, either presenting it as a more or less
connected whole, with a running commentary (as Mill
presented an account of Deductive Logic as a basis for
his Inductive Logic), or in what might be called the Built-
in Method, which incorporates the Aristotelian Logic
piecemeal into the symbolist system.[1]

Lastly, the student who wishes to form an idea of what
Symbolic Logic teaches apart from its discussion of
Aristotelian Logic can find out from a recent elementary
textbook, which works to the following programme: [2]
The Calculus of Propositions, the Axiomatic Method,
Elements of the Predicate Calculus, and Further Develop-
ments.

Under the first of these four headings certain common
modes of thinking, speaking, and arguing, namely, Contradiction (Negation), Conjunction, Disjunction, Implication,
Equivalence, and Alternation, are grouped together,
treated as the basic formal concepts for propositional
analysis, and translated into the symbolic notation, outlined above. The formal concepts in combination with
propositional variables yield ' Propositional Functions '.
A *matrix* or *truth-table* is then constructed for each propositional function, setting out the conditions under which
each function is true or false. In combination these
matrices or *truth-tables* form an instrument for testing the

---

[1] It may be questioned whether either method is a success educa-
tionally. The former method leaves the impression that Aristotelian
Logic is ' on its way out ', and the latter method destroys its unity
of structure. In my opinion the average, non-specialist student had
better learn Aristotelian Logic separately, and learn it first.

[2] *Introduction to Symbolic Logic* (1953), by A. H. Basson and D. J.
O'Connor.

validity of arguments. There are other methods, serving a similar purpose, which are known as 'Decision Procedures'.

The second section is an exercise in methodology, or formation of a system or scaffolding of argument. The Axiomatic Method aims at devising a system of abstract principles of inference, analogous to the definitions, postulates, and axioms of Euclidean geometry. The Axiomatic Method builds on a 'logical syntax', which gives the rules for using its symbols, as the laws of chess formulate the rules governing the use of the symbols (ivory, bone, or wooden) in which that game is carried out.

After the methodology we have another calculus. This time it is the Predicate Calculus, which breaks down the proposition into its constituent terms, and discusses their Quantity and Existential Import. In this it differs from the Propositional Calculus, which takes propositions as units under the symbols p, q, and r, and does not analyse them into terms.

The final section, as its title 'Further Developments' suggests, is of an indefinite character, and is meant to be introductory to the higher branches of Symbolic Logic. In it various supplementary problems are discussed, including the following: Formulae with more than one Quantifier, Two-termed Predicates, Satisfiability, Finite Domains, Infinite Domains, Logical Truth, Decision Procedures, and Axiom Systems.

INDEX

205